Nantucket Island

ROBERT GAMBEE

NANTUCKET ISLAND

W. W. Norton & Company
New York · London

For Claire, Frank and the others listed hereunder
who have helped me so much. This is their book:

Mimi Beman
Victoria Hawkins
Clay Lancaster
James Lentowski
Terry Pommett
Edouard Stackpole
John Welch

Library of Congress Cataloging in Publication Data
Gambee, Robert
Nantucket Island.

1. Nantucket Island (Mass.)–Description and travel–Views.
I. Title
F72.N2G17 1986   917.44'97'00222   86-8758

Printed in Japan
by Dai Nippon Printing Company Ltd.

Photographic consultation:
Peter C. Bunnell, Princeton University

Designed by Jacqueline Schuman

Frontispiece: The Old Mill, one of Nantucket's familiar landmarks, was built in 1746 and still grinds corn today. When the wind is right, canvas sails are added to the blades and the top of the mill is rotated to catch the breeze.

The Nantucket Historical Association and the Nantucket Conservation Foundation have been organized to conserve and preserve the valuable heritage we now have on Nantucket Island: the buildings and art created by men and women preceding us in history, and the land and vistas which are nature's gift. The combination is cherished by residents and visitors alike. We are pleased with this opportunity to share with you the unique beauty of our island, as captured by Robert Gambee's sensitive photographs.

The Historical Association was incorporated in 1894 to preserve knowledge of the Island's history for future generations and to convey the value of that history to visitors and residents, scholars and tourists. The Association administers thirteen properties, including the Whaling, Peter Foulger and Fair Street Museums, four historic houses, the Old Mill, and the Oldest House, all of which are open to the public. Through acceptance of facade easements, the NHA takes some responsibility for control over the outward appearance of historic structures, providing leadership in preservation of one of Nantucket's key attributes: our physical history. As a non-profit corporation, we encourage new memberships and donations to assist in carrying this important work forward.

The much younger and equally important Conservation Foundation plays a powerful role in protecting the island's open land. Founded in 1963, it presently owns and manages more than 6,000 acres, or 20% of all the land on Nantucket. Its goals are to preserve and protect for the public places of natural and historic significance, including beaches, moors, salt marshes, plains, and ponds. The Foundation is also a membership-supported, non-profit organization, accepting monetary donations and appropriate gifts of land to be saved from the ever-increasing pressures of development.

We have been given a magnificent treasure to enjoy, and we wish to see that it is preserved for others, too. It is this national heritage that our organizations jointly seek to protect for those following in our footsteps.

It is hoped that readers of this book will stroll leisurely through its pages, stopping now and again to rest at the many views of Nantucket homes, moors, ponds, and open spaces.

George A. Fowlkes, President
Nantucket Conservation Foundation, Inc.

H. Flint Ranney, President
Nantucket Historical Association

The lightship *Nantucket* is the largest lightship ever built. It was stationed for 40 years at the southern end of the Nantucket shoals and the eastern approach to the crowded shipping lanes to New York. This ship was built in 1936. The first lightship was a retired Nantucket whaler, painted red with yellow masts and named the *South Shoal*. It was placed in service in 1854 on the Davis Shoal, about 25 miles offshore. The whale lamps in the mastheads were visible for 15 miles on a clear evening. The *Nantucket* is owned and operated by the Nantucket Lightship Preservation, a nonprofit organization. Navigational buoys have taken the place of lightships today.

Harbor sights: The famous lightship *(left)*; the Yacht Club anchorage and a supervisor *(above)*.

Contents

Opposite: Rounding Brant Point. This is the site of the second lighthouse built in America (1746) after Boston's Beacon Light. Its familiar occulating red light indicates that it is on the starboard or right side of the channel, proceeding from seaward. A green beacon would have to be located on Coatue.

Catboats dozing in the morning light. As much a part of Nantucket as cobblestones and the Old Mill, the "Rainbow Fleet" consists of these wide-beamed, gaff-rigged catboats with colorful sails. Catboats have been popular since the 1880s on Nantucket because their large single sails provide great speed in smooth water and light wind.

One

The Faraway Island

My family first came to Nantucket almost fifty years ago. They wanted a place to get away to—something just a bit further away and lesser known. And they were right. When they got home friends asked about their summer on the Cape. They still do. Other friends have always confused Nantucket with the Vineyard.

It's interesting how little known the island really is. Yet one of its greatest treasures is its isolation. Being just a little further away and harder to get to has protected it over the years. While this book seeks to portray Nantucket as it appears today, one can never forget the tremendous history which it enjoys—unique, in many ways, from all other communities in America.

For this was an island that was once, and for almost a hundred years held the honor of being, the greatest whaling center in the world (surpassing even England which long ruled the waves). It was one of the most populous communities in the early days of our country and even was described as a "city at sea" by Daniel Webster in 1835. No other town in America today has as many homes (over eight hundred) built in the period 1740 to 1840, almost all of which are located in their original settings. During a hundred-year span, Orange Street was the home of over 125 whaling captains—a record of any such port in the country. At its peak, there were eighty-eight Nantucket whalers sailing around the world, often on voyages lasting two years or more. In fact, its only major bank, established in 1804, was appropriately named the Pacific Bank, not the New England or even the Atlantic Bank.

Then came the decline, and rapid it was. It began with the Great Fire in 1846, which eliminated a third of the town and, more important, vast stores of whale oil and related items in the warehouses. The California Gold Rush siphoned off many able-bodied sailors as did the Civil War. When the shifting sands made the harbor entrance unnavigable, things looked bad enough. But the discovery of petroleum and its refinement into kerosene put an end to the need for whale oil—the island's only major economy.

By 1870, hardly thirty years from the peak of prosperity, the town was an empty shell. Houses had no market value, no taxes were collected, and the island was badly in debt. The population was about a third of what it had been before. In retrospect it is fortunate that the decline was so swift and thorough. For the island was unable to experience even a small measure of the industrial revolution and the accompanying Victorian architecture that swept across the mainland.

Nantucket, which is the Indian term for "land far out to sea," has returned again out of the fog and past, waiting for you to discover it.

Above: Nantucket harbor from the steeple of Old North Church. The afternoon boat is just arriving from America. Scheduled steamer service began in 1818, and until the 1920s the boats were graceful sidewheelers with staterooms and dining salons. Presently the island is served by the *Nantucket* (1974), the *Uncateena* (1965 and lengthened in 1973), and the *Naushon* (1957), as well as two Hy-Line cruise vessels. Our beloved *Nobska* was retired in 1974 after almost 50 years of service.

The first ship built by the Nantucket Steamship Company was the *Telegraph* in 1832. Its hull was fortified to battle the ice and occasionally on winter runs passengers were asked to gather at the stern as the ship ran onto an ice floe. The passengers then moved to the bow and added their weight to that of the ship in breaking the ice. The first *Nantucket* was built in 1886 and the first *Uncateena* in 1902. These were both sidewheelers. The first propeller-driven steamship was the *Sankaty* in 1911.

Left: The view from the crow's nest of the *Nantucket* lightship, 68 feet above water. On the horizon is the steeple from which the panorama above was taken. At the left of center is the famous Wharf Rat Club and in the foreground are the North Wharf cottages and a fish shop.

Old North Wharf. This wharf is one of Nantucket's oldest, built in 1774. It is one of five wharves and a town pier but it is the only one that is residential. It is privately owned by individual families. The familiar gold-domed steeple of the Unitarian Church or South Tower may be seen in the photograph opposite. It was built in 1809 and is Nantucket's oldest church.

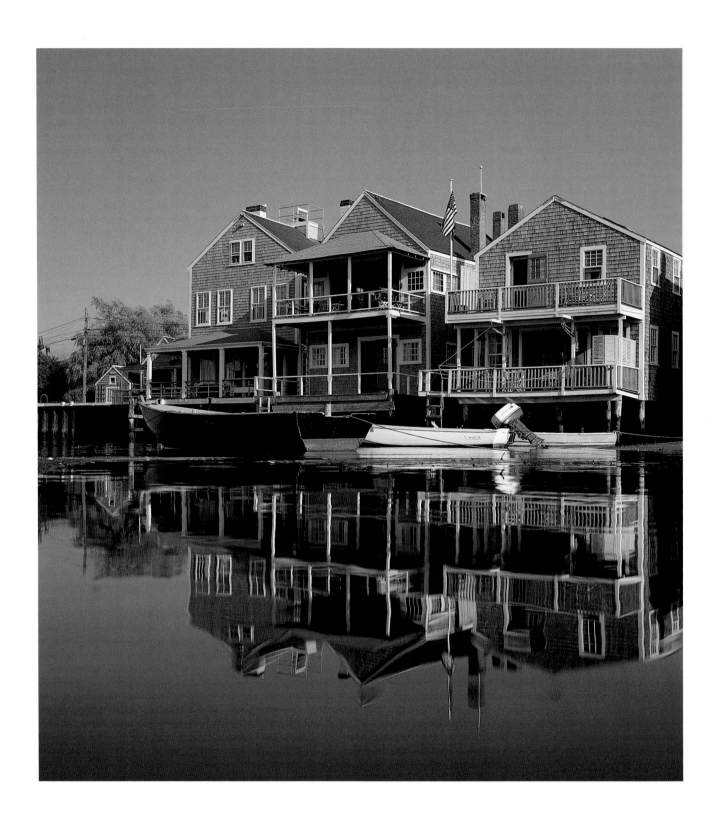

Burdett's Wharf was the name given to this section of lofts on North Wharf, many of which date from the 1850s. The view above was taken from the Skipper Restaurant, which was originally housed on an old coastal schooner. One of my brothers got his first summer job here in 1945.

The whalers are smaller now but the catch is still plentiful. These privately owned boats fish offshore and concentrate on cod, haddock, halibut, flounder, bluefish, and swordfish in the summer as well as sea scallops. Nantucket is best known for its bay scallops and offshore bluefish which are among the most abundant in the world. The market for scallops did not develop on the mainland until the 1880s. In 1881 scalloping began on Nantucket and soon it became the major livelihood for its winter residents, as they discovered the finest scalloping grounds in New England in the main harbor and also at Madaket.

An afternoon rest in the lee of the lightship.

North Wharf lofts lend an artistic flair to the harbor front. This is the only wharf where private residences are maintained, although Swain's Wharf now has cottages for overnight guests at the Marina.

Having a gam in the Wharf Rat Club *(above)*. This club *(opposite)* was founded in 1915. The clubhouse was originally a general store where men would sit around the potbellied stove and trade stories. The Wharf Rat Club has no bylaws, dues, or membership hierarchy. Acceptance is based on the ability to tell good tales.

Above: Travel to and from the ships in the harbor is by launch or rowboat.

Opposite, top: Summer reading *(Heidi* and *Charlotte's Web)* in one of the little North Wharf cottages on stilts. The wharf originally extended farther into the harbor and its stone foundation may still be seen at low tide.

Opposite, bottom: The harbor near Easy Street is the prettiest in New England.

The Hy-Line dock on a foggy morning. This is the successor to a company which began operations in 1946. It operates the *Brant Point* and *Point Gammon* motor vessels between Hyannis and Nantucket. Point Gammon is at the end of Great Island at Yarmouth.

The new terminal of the Steamship Authority *(left)* has replaced the familiar old structure built in 1929 *(below, left)*. The Woods Hole, Martha's Vineyard and Nantucket Steamship Authority is a public organization run by the communities it serves. New Bedford service was eliminated in 1960 and Hyannis added in 1972 although Hyannis service first began in the early 1830s. *Below*: On deck of the *Nantucket*, rounding Brant Point.

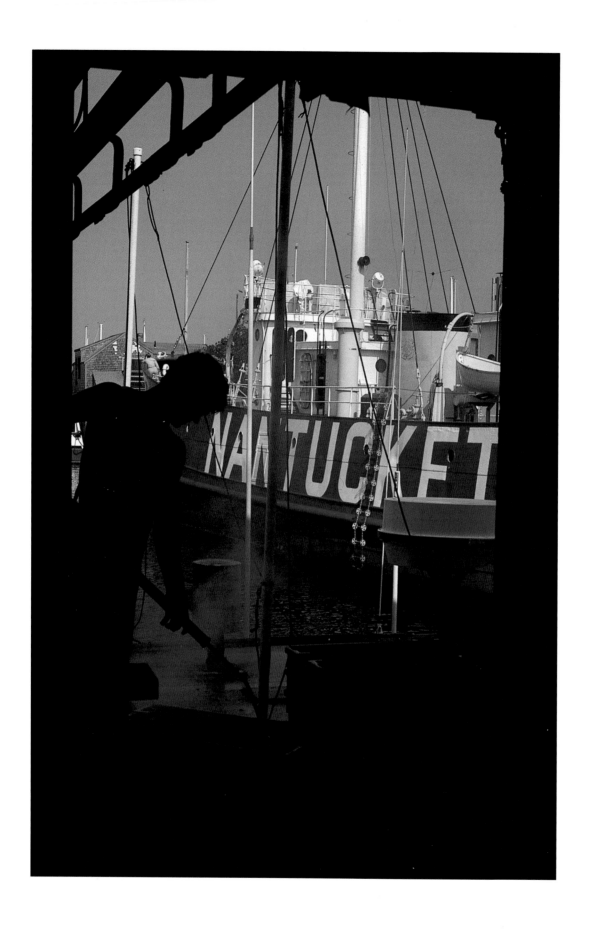

Two

The History of Nantucket

There were three factors that contributed to the unusual history of Nantucket: the whale, around which the island's entire economy revolved, taking its citizens to all the great seas of the globe and resulting in a prosperity that had few rivals on the mainland; the isolation of the sea; and the Quaker religion. The last provided the simple faith and stability that enabled Nantucketers to survive the whaling difficulties.

The story of Nantucket is like a play with three acts, each one ending with a major climax: the Revolution, the War of 1812, and the grand finale of the late 1840s. And everything was centered on whaling, which Nantucketers discovered by accident and were forced to pursue because there were no resources on the island. The land was sandy, had no wood to speak of, and was filled with hills, marshes, and swamps. Farming and sheep husbandry were tried (the sheep population in 1800 was about sixteen thousand) but weren't very profitable.

As early as 1730 Nantucket had twenty-five whalers. By 1840 there were over eighty Nantucket-owned brigs sailing around the world. There were five wharves in the harbor, thirty-six candle factories, rope walks, sail lofts, and shipyards. Almost everyone was connected with whaling—either going to sea directly or helping others to do so and waiting for their return. Because of their devotion to a single industry, these people became the most knowledgeable about whaling in the world. And this helps explain why Nantucket surpassed even the British, their only serious competitors, in this livelihood for many years. The British lacked the determination, energy (at least as far as whaling was concerned), and courage which Nantucket men were forced to assume. Whaling was their only business, whereas the British had commercial trade. The courage these people possessed is all but forgotten, most likely because we cannot fully appreciate what they were up against. The basic equation was: a group of sailors plus harpoon plus eighteen-foot whaleboat equals one whale (about a hundred feet or more in length). These animals were literally giants of the sea—among the largest animals in history. Their jaws were large enough and opened wide enough to consume the entire whaling party and boat in one piece. And they were not known for their tranquillity—especially when harpooned. The speed with which an angry whale could take the whalers for a "Nantucket sleigh ride" was frightening. Of greater concern was its diving or ramming either the whaleboat or the ship. In short, it was a risky and arduous profession.

Opposite: Swabbing the decks of a Harbor Square fish store.

The First Hundred Years

Nantucket was first sighted by Bartholomew Gosnold in 1602, when he was blown off course on his way from England to Virginia. It is fortunate he did not settle here because he might have subsequently chosen to name the island for himself. In 1635 the Earl of Sterling received a grant for the island from King Charles I, and in 1641 sold it to Thomas Mayhew, a Puritan merchant in Massachusetts.

In 1659 a group of nine men purchased the island from Thomas Mayhew Junior for thirty pounds and two hats. These non-Puritans sought refuge offshore from the bitter hostility that had arisen in Massachusetts against Baptists and Quakers. Thomas Macy had received a fine for giving shelter to some Quakers during a severe thunderstorm. Further assistance could have resulted in his being hanged. The original group of nine were: Thomas Barnard, Tristram and Peter Coffin, Christopher Hussey, Thomas Macy, William Pike, and John and Richard Swain. Before the purchase of the island was completed each member decided to take a partner, among whom were Edward and Nathaniel Starbuck. They were all planters who lived in Salisbury, a community north of Boston. Thomas and Sarah Macy were among the first to arrive in the fall of 1659. They sailed around Cape Cod and first settled at Madaket. By the next year, there were over sixty settlers (including Tristram and Dionis Coffin whose daughter, Mary Starbuck, was the first white child born on the island and a leader in organizing the regular monthly meetings of Friends). The next year they moved away from Madaket, which means "sandy soil," to more fertile sites between Capaum and Hammock Pond. The community was officially named Sherburne in 1673.

In the early 1700s the typical acre of Nantucket farmland yielded fifty bushels of corn. Fifty years later the yield was half of that due to poor soil conditions and overworked land. Farms on the mainland were yielding eighty to one hundred bushels an acre. Sheep raising was not much better; the animals were small and yielded little wool. Just before the Revolution there were over five thousand people on the island with only enough local produce to support ten percent of them. This forced the islanders to start plowing the sea around them at a much earlier stage than they would have had their land been the Napa Valley.

Whaling began when a whale strayed into the harbor and after several days was captured, although beached whales had been discovered before at Siasconset. By 1672 the islanders thought they should get a professional to teach them about whaling, and by 1690 they were off on a remarkable pursuit. In 1712, Chris Hussey came across a school of whales and in 1715 the farmers launched six ships cautiously seeking whales. Gradually they took longer and longer trips and by the turn of the century they were sailing around Cape Horn. The quest was for whale oil—primarily for England which consumed over four thousand tons of oil annually in homes and street lights. London was experiencing an epidemic of muggings and therefore decided to keep the street lamps burning all night.

In 1745 Nantucket merchants sent a load of whale oil to London and returned with a cargo of hardware, for the first time without going through the expense of a Boston broker. This episode convinced the islanders that they could become a leading whaling port and handle their own trading affairs without the assistance of off-island merchant bankers. Because of the close relationship between Nantucket and England, the former was granted a somewhat favorable status and, among other things, was exempted from the Massachusetts Restraining Bill of 1774 which restricted commerce elsewhere in New England.

In 1773, two Nantucket ships owned by William Rotch, the *Dartmouth* and the *Beaver*, were chartered in London by the East India Company to deliver a cargo of tea to Boston. While the cargo was subsequently dumped overboard on arrival by "Indians," none of the ships was affected. But when the American war broke out, Nantucket was not in an enviable position. Because of her dependence on Britain, she could offer neither resistance nor support and, as a result, her vessels were destroyed by both sides, depending on which group had issued a sailing permit. They were at the mercy of both the British Navy and the American privateers and, for a short while, tried to substitute other businesses (including cod fishing and farming).

But the island did not have enough food to feed itself nor enough firewood for fuel. By 1779 two-thirds of the families were out of firewood.

When the harbor froze during the cold winter of 1779-1780 people walked to Coatue and Coskata in search of juniper and cedar to burn. All usable timber on the island had been consumed by the end of the war. The hardship of the Revolution marks the end of act one of our story.

Rebuilding After the War

While most of her ships were destroyed in the war, those few that were left and able to sail were the first to fly the flag of the new United States overseas—in England in 1783, in Quebec, and various Spanish ports.

Gradually, Nantucket men accumulated a great familiarity with the seas. For example, they were the first to have intimate knowledge of the Gulf Stream. When Captain Timothy Folger plotted it for Benjamin Franklin (who was postmaster general at the time) in 1786, the sailing time to England was reduced by about two weeks. The British, considering themselves still the expert mariners, ignored the charts prepared by "those fishermen" and stuck to their traditional and more lengthy routes.

The end of act two of our story is climaxed with the War of 1812. By this time Nantucket had grown to a population of about seven thousand—including almost four hundred widows and as many fatherless children. Between the British blockade and the seizure of her vessels by both the British and the French Navy (many Nantucket sailors were impressed into French service), life was pretty grim. Over half the whaling fleet was destroyed in the war, and the island was thrown into a severe depression which lasted for over three years. But due to the characteristic faith and endurance of the islanders, by 1822 the island had tripled the size of its fleet and restored the whaling industry to its former level (at the same time the British whaling business was floundering). This marks the beginning of the third and final act.

The Greatest Whaling Center in the World

Beginning in the 1820s and building up in the two succeeding decades, the Nantucket whaling economy grew rapidly. Herman Melville was struck by the courage and strength of the whalers who set forth alone from their little elbow of sand located away offshore. "And thus have these naked Nantucketers," as he described them in *Moby Dick*, "these sea-hermits, issuing from their anthill in the sea, overrun and conquered the watery world like so many Alexanders; parcelling out among them the Atlantic, Pacific, and Indian Oceans, as the three pirate powers did Poland. Let America add Mexico to Texas, and pile Cuba upon Canada; let the English overswarm all India, and hang out their blazing banner from the sun; two-thirds of this terraqueous globe are the Nantucketer's. For the sea is his; he owns it, as Emperors own empires; other seamen having but a right of way through it." As early as 1824 men like Captain George Chase were returning home with as much whale oil as England's entire consumption several years before. (Chase's haul was over three thousand barrels of oil after a three year voyage.) Eight years later (1832) over thirty whaling ships set out to sea in one year alone. By 1843, Nantucket had eighty-eight whalers out sailing around the world. But by this time the voyages were long and hard. The sailors' home was their ship and most of their time was spent in the forecastle, a rather dark and gloomy area below. Food consisted of a mixture of tea, coffee, and molasses, or another dish called "scouse," consisting of hard tack, beans, and meat. Captain Benjamin Worth *(143)* spent forty-one years at sea, making thirty-four voyages in all. He is said to have sailed over a million miles, rounded the Horn sixteen times, brought in over nineteen thousand barrels of oil, and never lost a man. The total amount of time he spent at home in forty-one years was about six years.

George W. Gardner went to sea at the age of thirteen for about the same number of years as Captain Worth. He was a master for half the period. Married at twenty-nine and father of fifteen children, he spent less than five years at home in the aggregate. In 1812, he was taken by the British and lost everything. In 1820, the *Essex* was rammed and sunk by an angry whale, forcing

Captain George Pollard (57) and a handful of survivors to spend three months in an open lifeboat. This bleak story is thought to have been the basis for *Moby Dick*.

As the photographs in this book demonstrate, whaling for those who were fortunate and determined was rewarding. Joseph Starbuck began building the "Three Bricks" for his sons in 1836 at a cost of more than $40,000—an amount that seemed scandalous at the time (116 to 119). William Hadwen built two Greek Revival houses across the street. He predicted they would make people talk, and he was right. One had an upstairs ballroom with a sprung floor and a domed roof that opened to the stars (123). Nearby, the William Crosbys gave elaborate dinner parties at their One Pleasant Street home (167) where they introduced frozen mousse and other new dishes.

The elaborate houses that Starbuck and Hadwen were building stirred the competitive juices of Jared Coffin. His large, brick walled estate at the edge of town was no longer suitable (168). He decided to build the largest and tallest house on the island in 1845, so large that its immediately succeeding owner turned it into a hotel.

Lower Main Street, formerly called State Street, was originally paved with cobblestones in 1837. These came over as ballast from the mainland (or America, as it is commonly referred to by Nantucketers even today). While this was done for utilitarian purposes, enabling the heavy oil carts to move up from the wharves without sinking into the mud, the paving of Upper Main Street in 1852 was for more aesthetic reasons. In addition, the great elm trees that line the street were planted by the Coffins about this time.

The good years in act three lasted only until the late 1840s. Then began the downfall, starting first with an enormous fire in 1846 which destroyed thirty-six acres of town buildings, homes, shops, and most important, whale oil and related items stored in warehouses. There was a brief period of rebuilding, but it was like the brilliant color of the maple tree before it drops its leaves and becomes dormant. Whaling became less successful. In 1846 the *Peru* returned with 966 barrels of oil, in 1847 the *Mary* with 862, and in 1848 the *Henry* with only 482—this compared with the *Sarah*'s haul of 3,492 barrels eighteen years earlier. In 1849, most of the better sailors decided prospecting for gold would be more profitable than for whale oil. A few years later, The Civil War siphoned off additional men. Beginning in the 1840s, the strip of sand known as the Nantucket Bar had blocked the harbor entrance to such an extent that whalers could not cross even with the help of "camels"—specially designed cradles with pontoons that floated the ships high in the water. In 1854, a Waltham group began to produce petroleum oil commercially, the supply of which was guaranteed in 1859 when the first petroleum well was drilled in Pennsylvania. By 1869, Nantucket's last whalers set sail, and an era had ended.

Looking up Main Street past the Nantucket Looms and Buttner's. Nantucket's magnificent Main Street, the heart of downtown, was laid out in 1697 and until the early 1800s was called State Street. When Straight Wharf was built by Richard Macy in 1723 as an extension of the street, the whaleships were provided direct access to the shops and fitters. This was an unusual feature, as was the width of the street.

Cobblestones were laid down beginning in 1831, enabling the heavy carts to move up to the stores more easily. The cobbles were brought over from the mainland as ballast in the whaleships. The elm trees of lower Main Street are among the most spectacular in all of New England.

The Pacific Club, 1772, originally the counting house of William Rotch and Sons. One room became the first Customs Office in America, with operations continuing from 1783 until 1913. The sign on the building bears the names *Beaver*, *Dartmouth*, and *Bedford*—all Rotch ships. The first two were involved in the Boston Tea Party, and the third was the first ship to fly the new flag of the United States in any British port. The Pacific Club, initially a group of retired whaling captains, acquired the building in 1861.

At the opposite end of Main Street is the Pacific Bank, founded in 1804 *(above)*. The handsome brick building, with stone steps leading up to a fan-lit entrance with Ionic columns, was built in 1818. The horse fountain *(right)* was given by William Hadwen Starbuck in 1885. It serves as a reminder of the importance of horses in the pre-automotive era.

The Bartlett Farm stand on Main Street has been offering freshly picked vegetables and flowers at this location for over 35 years. The Bartlett Farm is Nantucket's largest, with over 100 acres under cultivation. It has been in the family for seven generations.

Looking out on Main Street Square from the Nantucket Pharmacy. Both the pharmacy and the Ford date from 1938. Prior to this the A & P was located here.

The intersection of Main and Orange Streets *(left)* and the Dreamland Theatre *(above)*. The landmark Dreamland is Nantucket's oldest and largest theatre, the only structure on South Water Street that predates the 1846 fire. The building was originally constructed in 1829 at the corner of Main Street and Ray's Court. It has been a straw hat factory, a Friends' meeting house, and a rollerskating rink, and in 1883 was moved to Brant Point to become the centerpiece of the Nantucket, the island's grandest hotel. In 1906 it was floated back to its present location and became a theatre.

Above: The north side of Main Street. *Right*: My earliest childhood memory is of standing on this corner near the Hub the day the skies were raining paper. I didn't know what the occasion was at the time but many years later realized it was VJ Day. The soldier in this photograph was celebrating too, somewhere over there, and as for the woman taking the raffle ticket for the lightship basket —maybe she was the little girl standing near us on the sidewalk that day.

Main Street shops change very little over the years. Congdon's Pharmacy was selling tickets to 'Sconset Casino performances in 1901. The photograph above was taken almost 20 years ago. My Nantucket convertible is parked in the foreground. It is the one with the handlebar basket.

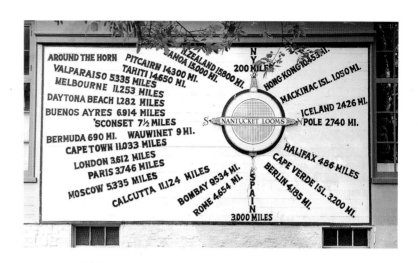

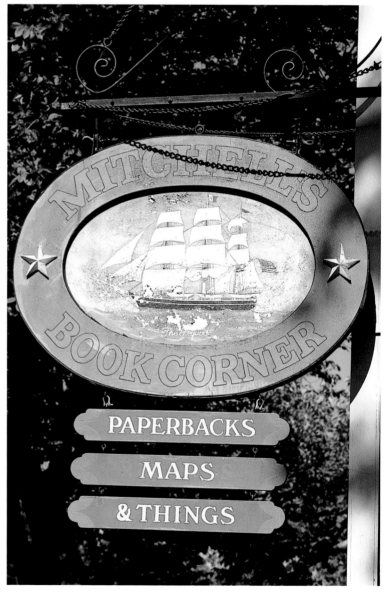

Nantucket signs at the Looms *(above)* and Mitchell's *(right)*. The familiar compass has been pointing the way to Wauwinet and New Zealand (and points in between) since it was first painted on the side of Gardner's Gift Shop in the 1920s.

In Nantucket everyone reads. For some it's a
Benchley classic *(above)* and for others it's
Mother Goose (right).

The Whaling Museum on Broad Street *(above, left, and opposite)* was built by William Hadwen and his partner, Nathaniel Barney, in 1847 as a candle factory. Everything on Broad Street was destroyed in the Great Fire of 1846 except for the Jared Coffins' house. Broad Street was originally laid out in 1678, and like its sister Main Street, it was widened after the fire. Also like its sister, Broad Street has cobblestones, now quietly napping under a blanket of macadam. The Old Town Building *(above, right)*, 2 Union Street, was built *ca.* 1830 for Thomas Coffin and James Athearn. It presently houses the administrative offices of the Nantucket Historical Association, incorporated on July 9, 1894.

The Museum Shop offers a wide variety of handmade, New England gifts. It is considered to be among the finest museum gift shops in the country, and the proceeds from its operation go directly to the Nantucket Historical Association.

49

The inside of the famous Pacific Club *(left)* where members have gathered since 1861 to play cribbage, have a gam, or just sit and "watch the pass" on Main Street. The Peter Foulger Museum *(above)*, adjacent to the Whaling Museum, is patterned after the Coffin School *(opposite)*.

The Coffin School, founded in 1827 by Admiral Sir Isaac Coffin for descendants of Tristam Coffin. A small tuition was charged because anything free was often doubted. The fine Greek Revival building on Winter Street was built in 1852.

Most Nantucket buildings are very old, such as the Savings Bank on Orange Street *(opposite, bottom)*. Some however are of recent construction, such as Zero Main Street *(above)* and 23 Federal Street *(opposite, top)* but blend into their environments because of the regulations of the Nantucket Historic Districts Commission. Restoration work began in the 1920s and received further impetus from a 1940 survey by Everett Crosby, who recommended a general policy that the old was to be preserved, the garish avoided, and commercialism disguised. Edouard Stackpole returned from directorship of the Mystic Seaport and published stories of Nantucket history in the Historical Association bulletins. Walter Beinecke began to develop the waterfront and Marina in the 1960s through Sherbune Associates, which is housed at Zero Main Street.

The Nantucket Atheneum on India Street. This is the island's public library and was built in 1847. The architect was Frederick Brown Coleman, who left his mark on Nantucket in the 1840s. He designed the impressive Greek Revival houses at 94 and 96 Main Street in 1840–1845, the First Baptist Church in 1841, and added the massive Ionic portico to the earlier Methodist Church in 1840.

The Atheneum is Coleman's masterpiece. Its facade is impressive and monumental—windowless like a Greek temple. It has double pediments on the south, one embracing the entire portico pediment. The two Ionic columns make a statement that is both elegant and bold.

Steamboat Wharf shops. This wharf was originally constructed in 1772 and has always been a principal point of debarkation. Young's Cycle Shop has been a familiar tenant of long standing on the wharf.

The Downy Flake *(above)* and the Seven Seas Gifts *(right)* are part of Nantucket lore. The Seven Seas was originally the home of Captain William Brock. It was also the home of Captain George Pollard, whose *Essex* was rammed by an angry whale in 1820 causing him and a few survivors to spend three months in an open lifeboat. Herman Melville is thought to have based *Moby Dick* on this incident.

Nantucket symbols—a figurehead that once may have graced the bow of a whaleship, and an elegant voluted Ionic capital of the Atheneum. One represents the means of the island's early prosperity and the other represents the results.

Right: Old South Wharf (1770), a wharf of studios and galleries. *Below*: A clothing shop at the entrance to Old North Wharf (1774).

Opposite, above: Colorful silkscreens and watercolors in South Wharf galleries. *Opposite, right*: A Canadian artist on Easy Street.

Lightship basket-makers in their workshops at home and aboard the lightship. Baskets were originally made by the Indians, and by the 1830s began to have wooden bottoms rather woven ones. Nantucketers started to use rattan from the Philippines and China, which they imported directly. A third characteristic was also added at this time: the use of molds to make perfectly round nests of baskets. Beginning in 1856 baskets were made on the *South Shoal* lightship by sailors who, during their long periods of isolation, created some fine examples. One of the most prolific makers was Captain Charles Ray, who had completed 200 by 1866. His grandson Mitchell carried on the tradition, and after signing the bottom of the basket, added the following verse: *"I was made on Nantucket, I'm strong and I'm stout. Don't lose me or burn me and I'll never wear out."* José Formoso Reyes came to Nantucket from the Philippines in 1945 and, unable to obtain a teaching position, took up basket-making. He was a skilled craftsman, adding the lid to the baskets and the familiar ivory carving. By the 1950s the present-day basket, a familiar badge recognized by fellow Nantucketers around the world, had evolved.

A Nantucket portrait painter at work in her West Chester Street studio. Nantucket offers endless opportunities to her artists for painting people, moors, ships, or Main Street.

The shops on Main Street *(above and opposite)*. This section is also known as Main Street Square. It is a tribute to the Nantucket Historic Districts Commission that there are no neon signs on the island and not a single traffic light anywhere.

Nantucket giftshops at Harbor Square *(right, top)*, on Main Street *(right, bottom)*, Straight Wharf *(opposite, top,)* and Centre Street *(opposite, bottom)*. The Nantucket Looms offers hand-knitted clothing and fabric by the yard. The Four Winds was once the Old Blacksmith Shop *(ca. 1855)*. The shops on Centre Street (laid out in 1678) were originally run by women, and the stretch from Liberty to India Streets is still referred to as Petticoat Row.

Summer dining is a delightful experience, whether it be a fancy French restaurant, a pub with long tables of newly made friends, or the Sweet Shop.

Nantucket shops on Broad Street *(above)*, Main and South Water Streets *(opposite)*. On the second floor of Upstairs Downstairs was located the *Mirror*, an island newspaper founded in 1845 and consolidated with the *Inquirer* in 1865. The latter started in 1821 and is one of the oldest continuously published newspapers in the country. When I was growing up it still had a large blanket format and required long arms to hold it open.

The shops on Main Street, Centre Street, and Old South Wharf glow with hospitality on a summer evening. There is no harsh neon or blinking light to attract the stroller's attention.

One of the island's oldest giftshops is Coffin's on Main Street, whose principal attractions are painted on the storefront and reflect the light of the nearby street lamps.

Three

The Island Today

Today Nantucket still enjoys its insularity and pride. All-digit dialing, cable television, and jet plane service now connect it with America, but only on a temporary basis. All you have to do is visit the airport on a densely foggy Sunday afternoon—hearing the crowds cheer as each plane lands or takes off, as if a touchdown had been scored—to realize how isolated the island can really be.

But once you're there, it's like no other place. Over fifty-five miles of broad clean beaches encircle the small island. The water is often warmer than Long Island's south shore, thanks to the Gulf Stream. Crisscrossing the ten thousand acres of moors are miles of paths and unpaved roads taking the hiker through fields of heather, holly, and Scotch broom *(247 to 251)*. The island is inhabited by deer, pheasant, quail, and rabbits (by the thousands), but interestingly there are no squirrels or chipmunks. Scattered among the hills are fresh water ponds filled with perch and pickerel and surrounded by wintergreen, Virginia creeper, and rugosa roses *(232 to 246)*. These ponds are the work of a glacier which originally formed Nantucket as a moraine and later became an island when rising waters filled the coastal plains. Offshore are bluefish and striped bass for the surf casters, especially at Madaket, as well as scallops for hardy souls in winter.

For those who find the lazy pace of Nantucket town too taxing, there's Madaket to the west and 'Sconset to the east. Madaket means "sandy soil at the end of the land" and 'Sconset, where beached whales were commonly found, means "place of many whale bones." Quidnet ("at the point") was established as a refuge for the escapees from the urban ills of 'Sconset, and then there's Wauwinet (named for an Indian chief)—a community for those who would really prefer to be on a separate island but enjoy being connected with the rest of the world. Polpis, Quaise, Shimmo, and Monomoy ("divided harbor," "tall reeds," "a spring," and "rich earth," respectively) form little pockets of homes along the harbor shoreline like so many Greenwiches and Dariens—but this is no Fairfield County. This is sleepy Nantucket, one of the few entities in the country that's both town and county (not to mention an island). Tuckernuck and Muskeget, two privately owned islands which unfortunately are not open to visitors, Esther, a newly formed island named after a hurricane, and Whale are all quietly anchored off Nantucket's west coast *(306 to 311)*. Tuckernuck means "loaf of bread" and was once nothing but farmland, connected to Nantucket by a sandy road. Once upon a time and not so long ago, so the story goes, an elderly Coffin farmer drove his wagonload of produce into the town market and on his return that afternoon found that Tuckernuck had broken away. He eventually got home all right . . . by boat. Muskeget ("grassy land"), on the other hand, has always been an island and therefore is less developed with houses and roads than its neighbor. The lonely building on the southern shore near the cove entrance was once a "humane house" and is one of the oldest still standing on Nantucket. Manned by volunteers on rotating shifts, the humane houses launched rescue squads for ships endangered on Nantucket shoals and offered shelter for the shipwrecked.

There are three golf courses on the island which often present a unique handicap in the late afternoon (especially at Sankaty Head and 'Sconset)—as the fog rolls across the fairways, play must be suspended until it temporarily lifts *(201)*. On the way to either of these courses, you'll drive alongside one of the first bikeways built in this country *(290 and 291)*. On a summer day, it's busy with a wide assortment of cyclists and their machines—racers, lightweights, tandems, three wheelers for those who can't ride, and occasionally a bicycle for three or four for those who don't know any better.

Lower Main Street is the scene of activity early on a summer morning, before beach time. Rows of Jeepsters and aging jalopies line both sides or form a circling parade as passengers spill out to pick up the paper or fresh flowers and vegetables *(38 and 39)*. While waiting at the Hub for your Sunday paper, which often may not arrive until Monday evening, you'll notice an interesting collection of people: children with ice cream cones, Boston Brahmins in their worn-out sneakers, and Nantucket women of all ages sporting lightship baskets. These baskets, once made during the long shifts at the lighthouses and lightships, are now the pride of Nantucket ladies, including the "regular" off-islanders *(62)*. These baskets are equally at home at the A & P and the Yacht Club. They travel to the beach every day, are rained on, and even occasionally sat on, and, generally, under such "normal" conditions, they last forever.

The sounds of Nantucket are gentle: bicycles jiggling on Main Street's cobbles, waves lapping the sides of a wooden hull, a sail luffing in the breeze, a little voice calling "Hi, Grandma," from the arriving steamer and a dozen grandmothers waving "Hello, dear" from the wharf, the birds chirping during the day, and the lull of the crickets and fog horns in the evening . . . a stillness and calm that tranquillizes everyone and encourages them to leave all of their cares behind for a while.

By 9:00 P.M. the old Lisbon bell in South Tower *(179)* begins its sounding of the curfew as it has regularly done since 1849. Every evening it strikes fifty-two times—no one really knows why anymore but that doesn't matter since it's always been that way. And that's the story of Nantucket. Nothing ever changes much there, and no one really would want it to.

Opposite: A three-masted schooner at anchor. Schooners have two or more masts, with the taller mainmast behind the smaller foremast. A yawl has two masts with the mainmast in front, and a sloop has only one mast. During the year the island receives many such visitors. There are approximately 200 moored in the harbor on a busy August day. One of the largest private sailing vessels to visit the island was the 170' *Seven Seas*, a three-masted schooner built in 1928.

Nantucket boats, like toy boats in a bathtub *(above)*. However, these are for the big boys with prices starting well into six figures. To accommodate many of them, Walter Beinecke built a marina in 1967 which now has 245 slips *(right)*. On an average summer day 40–60 slips may be vacated for new tenants, keeping the wharfinger busy.

81

The Marina offers an attractive setting for sailors and observers. There are also cottages on Swain's Wharf for those who wish to spend a few nights ashore. Obed Swain was the wharfinger when it was reconstructed in 1850. The wharf was originally built by Zenas Coffin and Sons in 1816 and extended in 1831. It has a solid foundation of granite blocks brought from Connecticut, the only Nantucket wharf so constructed. Charles and Henry Coffin had a brick warehouse at the foot of the wharf, which more recently has served as the American Legion headquarters.

Cottages on stilts, an old Cape Cod catboat, and the sunlit sparkle of the harbor's water are all gentle reminders of Nantucket's nautical past.

Beetle cats near Swain's Wharf. Catboats have been popular on Buzzard's Bay and Nantucket Sound since the 1880s. They have a center-board hull, a wide beam, and a single, large gaff sail. Originally they were used for lobstering and hand lining fishing along the shore. At the turn of the century the *Lilian*, a 40-foot catboat, ferried passengers from Straight Wharf to Wauwinet and back.

The Easy Street harbor was once called "Catboat Basin." Shown in the photograph is a "Rainbow" or beetle cat, setting off on a harbor sail. The "Rainbow Fleet" has been a Nantucket institution since the turn of the century. Most of the boats have been built by the Crosby family of Osterville.

Nantucket pinks: eventide in the harbor. All is quiet now and the visitors are preparing for a night ashore—dinner at the Mad Hatter or maybe the Jared Coffin House, and then an overnight at one of the wharf cottages.

89

Above: Dusk is a special time on the island as the warm light of a setting sun or the lamps on shore are reflected in the deep blue of water and sky. It is the short period between sunset and darkness that is difficult but rewarding to capture on film. *Opposite*: Silver sequens glisten in Easy Street harbor.

The view of the harbor at sundown from Monomoy. *Above:* Brant Point's familiar red light may be seen on the horizon. *Right:* the lights of the town glow like Christmas lights in the snow.

From Coatue or Monomoy the Nantucket sunset and afterglow are special sights. Monomoy means "rich soil" and Coatue means "at the pine tree place."

This dramatic sunset shows the familiar South Tower
in a fiery light seen with a telephoto lens from Shimmo,
which is the Indian word for "a spring."

The William Hadwen houses, 94 and 96 Main Street (1840–1845). These Greek Revival houses, built by a wealthy silversmith and merchant, are the most dramatic of the Main Street homes. Note the unusual Corinthian capitals of No. 94—the only such capitals on the island. The entablature above has bold dentils and modillions. The style of No. 96 with its simpler Ionic moldings is a bit quieter. Hadwen lived at No. 96 and his niece, Mary Swain, at No. 94.

Four

Nantucket Architecture

Nantucket is an architectural miracle. Its houses sit side by side, each a bit different from the next, and none clamoring for attention. They were all built on an island thirty miles at sea without native trees large enough for structural timbers or flooring. Everything was imported, and great care was taken to get it right the first time, to maintain, and occasionally to relocate. The island is one of the largest and finest historic districts in America.

Several distinctions may be made about these homes. First, many have a unique glass transom over the interior doors, probably to detect fires. And since the fire was the chief source of light and warmth, they were a constant presence and threat. Second, is the rooftop walk which was used either to spot incoming whaleships or to enable a busy seaman's wife to pour a bucket of sand down a burning chimney. And third, is both the absence of the overhang, which was popular elsewhere on early New England homes, and the absence of the popular Cape Cod cottage which sprang up throughout the Northeast.

A stroll along upper Main Street offers an architectural experience unparalleled anywhere else in New England. All of the homes on this street were built with whale oil. Most of the wealth was accumulated by the whale merchants and investors rather than the captains themselves. Zenas Coffin and Joseph Starbuck were two such men, and between them they account for thirteen of the most prominent Main Street residences. Zenas Coffin was one of the wealthiest men in America at the turn of the nineteenth century. His sons lived at Nos. 75 and 78 Main Street, while his daughters occupied Nos. 90, 91, and 99 and granddaughters Nos. 86 and 98. Joseph Starbuck built three matching brick houses for his sons, Nos. 93, 95, and 97, while his daughters lived across the street at Nos. 92, 96, and 100.

The Macys were not to be outdone by such display. Francis, George, Silvanus, Thomas, and Zaccheus all lived along the street (Nos. 77, 86, 89, 99, and 107, respectively), although it should be noted that Thomas married a Zenas Coffin girl and George a Zenas Coffin granddaughter.

The original Nantucket settlement was at Sherburne, between Capaum Pond and Hummock Pond. Capaum was open to the north shore at the time and afforded a protected harbor. When a storm closed it off in the latter part of the eighteenth century, the inhabitants gradually moved to a new site called Wesco, which is approximately where Nantucket is today. Because of the tremendous scarcity of wood, many houses were simply picked up and relocated; it was cheaper to move than to build. (In fact, Herman Melville observed in *Moby Dick* that Nantucketers carried their wood around as if it were pieces of the true cross.)

The Elihu Coleman house, built in 1722 *(135)*, is the only homestead remaining on its original site in Sherburne. The Christian house of 1720 *(140)* was moved into town in its entirety in 1741 by its owner Thomas Macy who then gave it to his son Nathaniel. Similarly, the eastern section of the Christopher Starbuck house *(131)* is thought to have been built in Sherburne in 1690. The western half dates from around 1715. Sections of the Zaccheus Macy house *(134)* and the Joshua Coffin house *(151)* were also brought over from Sherburne.

Captain Richard Gardner's home, built in 1724 *(138)*, is located on what used to be the main road between Sherburne and Wesco. Note the similarities in style between this and the Elihu Coleman house mentioned earlier. Both retain the central chimney originally incorporated in the houses of the mid- to late seventeenth century. (See the Jethro Coffin house of 1686, *136 and 137.*) While the Coleman and Gardner houses have added second stories on the front, they still retain the steep shed roof to the north—facing south with their backs to the north wind.

The Jethro Coffin house has become known as the "Oldest House," although both "Shanunga" *(271)* and "Auld Lang Syne" *(274)* in 'Sconset are believed to predate it. This house was built as a wedding present for Jethro and his bride, Mary Gardner, by their respective fathers. The materials came from Peter Coffin's timberlands and sawmill at Exeter, New Hampshire. The house was meant to be something special. The massive central chimney, large fireplaces, and lean-to style were characteristic of the time. It is extraordinary to realize this house is now three hundred years old.

As the community moved eastward and began to settle at Wesco, the houses were located closer together and right on the street, in the English style. This is in contrast to other New England towns where houses often were set back behind lawns or gardens. As a result, Nantucket developed quickly into a city as opposed to a village. Even at the peak of whaling prosperity, Nantucketers preferred to build their stately homes right next to one another as they might have done in New York or Philadelphia. In fact, Jared Coffin's wife was so unhappy about being stuck out at "Moor's End," completed in 1834 *(168 to 170)* that she convinced him to build a house closer to town, which he did in 1845 *(171 to 174)*.

Proceeding up Main Street from the Pacific Bank, one notices two prominent homes, both of which were occupied by presidents of the bank. No. 72 Main Street *(105)* was built by John Wendell Barret in 1820. This dignified house barely survived the Great Fire of 1846, not because the flames were about to engulf it but because the fire wardens intended to blow it up to check the fire's spread. Mrs. Barrett simply refused to leave and fortunately the direction of the fire changed, sparing the house. Frederick Mitchell built the house opposite at 69 Main Street *(106)* in 1834. He was a whaling merchant and also was president of the bank.

Henry and Charles Coffin, sons of Zenas Coffin, built the identical houses at 78 and 75 Main Street between 1831 and 1833 *(107)*. Charles was a Quaker and preferred the conservative brownstone trim, whereas Henry had white trim and a cupola instead instead of an exposed roof walk. The two brothers were quite philanthropic, planting the elm trees on Main Street in 1851 and bringing a wide variety of wildlife to the island at about the same time (including over forty thousand English pine trees).

The rooftop walk, like the one on the Sidney Chase house at 82 Main Street *(110)*, was an essential part of Nantucket architecture, enabling the women to watch for the return of their sailing husbands. They have often been called "widows' walks" which is a mistake because clearly if a woman were indeed a widow she would have no need to be up there. George Macy lived at 86 Main Street *(111)* in a house built by his wife's grandfather, Zenas Coffin, in 1834. His uncle, Matthew Crosby, a successful whaler and subsequent ship owner and merchant, lived in the Federalist house at 90 Main Street *(112)*, which was built in 1829. Note the similarity between this and Thomas Macy II's house at 99 Main Street, built two years before in 1827 *(127)*. Both Crosby and Macy married Zenas Coffin girls. Captain Job Coleman lived at 88 Main Street *(111)*, a home which dates from about 1830. He was one of the first to sail for California in 1849 at the beginning of the famous rush for gold.

Across the street are two houses dating from the early 1800s. Silvanus Macy, a prominent whale fitter and brother of Obed Macy, lived at No. 89, the original portion of which dates from 1740 *(113)*, while Henry Swift and his bride (another Zenas Coffin girl) lived happily at No. 91 *(115)*.

The three identical houses located at Nos. 93, 95, and 97 Main Street *(116 to 119)* are commonly referred to as the "Three Bricks." They were built between 1836 and 1838 by Joseph Starbuck for his three sons, William, Matthew, and George at a cost of $40,000 which seemed almost scandalous at the time. Matthew's house, the "Middle Brick," still remains in the family. Joseph Starbuck's daughters lived directly opposite the "Three Bricks" at Nos. 92, 96, and 100. The first of these houses was built in 1838 by William Swain. The second, along with its companion next door, No. 94, was constructed between 1840 and 1845 by William Hadwen, a silversmith, whale oil merchant, and a candle maker *(122 to 125)*. The refined Greek style of these houses, which were designed by Frederick Brown Coleman, represents the zenith of whaling prosperity. No. 94 has a second floor ballroom with a specially sprung dance floor and a rooftop dome that can be opened to the stars. William Hadwen and his partner, Nathaniel Barney, originally lived in a two family house at No. 100 *(129)*, the rear portion of which dates from the early 1700s. This home was later occupied by Joseph Mitchell, who was a whaler and a "'49er." Hadwen also built and operated, with Barney, the brick candle factory now housing the Whaling Museum *(47)*. In between the two Hadwen homes lived Jared Coffin's son, Benjamin, who like his father was also a whale oil merchant. This dignified house was built in 1836 *(127)* and has an accompanying sidewalk paved with bluestone. The James Bunker house at No. 102 *(133)* is believed to be one of the first houses in Nantucket built of two stories from front to back. It dates from about 1740.

Zaccheus Macy, grandson of Thomas Macy, one of the island's first settlers, lived in the house at 107 Main Street *(134)*, thought to have been built in 1748. Zaccheus was a prominent whaler and boat builder. On the side, he was an expert setter of broken bones, having studied the subject extensively in his youth. It is estimated that he set about two thousand bones during his lifetime (all for free).

The Peter Folger II house on Center Street *(144)*, built in 1750, was occupied by Folgers for almost two hundred years. Peter I was a grandfather of Benjamin Franklin. The unusual third story was added in 1815.

The second story design of Job Macy's house on Mill Street, also completed in 1750, was such a radical departure from the accepted lean-to look that his father, a strict Quaker, vowed never to enter it. And he kept his word. Around the corner at 15 Pleasant Street lived Nantucket's first historian, Obed Macy *(151)*. He was also a shipfitter and builder, in partnership with his brother, Silvanus. There were three generations of Macy partnerships in this business, continuing with their respective sons, Thomas and Peter, and grandsons Isaac and Philip. Another grandson of Silvanus (and grandnephew of Obed) was Rowland H. Macy who started a dry goods business in New York.

Maria Mitchell was born in the house on Vestal Street subsequently named for her *(157)*. It was built in 1790. Her father never attended college but nevertheless was an overseer of Harvard (the standards were lower in those days). He was also a cashier at the Pacific Bank on whose roof she had her observatory. Maria became one of our foremost astronomers and a professor at Vassar.

While Orange Street *(163)* boasted the reputation of being home to 126 whaling captains, it was Pleasant Street that rivaled Main Street for expression of whaling wealth. John Coleman designed the two graceful homes at Nos. 7 and 9 during the early 1820s *(166)*. His brother, Frederick, designed the Greek Revival mansions on Main Street about twenty years later, as well as the Baptist and Methodist Churches and the Atheneum, the last being probably his greatest achievement *(180, 181, 55)*. Both architects were noted for their excellent taste, proportionate designs, and their carving and finishing skills. They were two of the most influential men to shape the face of Nantucket. William Crosby and his wife lived at One Pleasant Street *(167)*, a home which was completed in 1837. It became known as Nantucket's "social center," with the Crosbys entertaining regularly. The house was decorated with marble mantlepieces, French doors, and silver doorknobs.

"Moor's End" was built between 1829 and 1834 by Jared Coffin *(168 to 170)*, who had accumulated a fortune through partnerships in three successful whaleships. As previously mentioned, Mrs. Coffin felt it was too far out of town and convinced him to build another home in town in 1845 *(171 to 174)*. A year later they packed up and moved to Boston, again most likely at her request. "Moor's End" was sold and resold many times. Finally in 1873 it was put up for auction and Jared Gardner bought it for $2,350. (He also bought the Old Mill in 1822 for twenty dollars and was going to use it for firewood, but later changed his mind when he saw how difficult it would be to take apart.) "Moor's End" is probably the island's most beautiful home, and it was practically given away—an indication of the extreme poverty which had befallen the island at that time. While the values of this and other fine homes were unusually depressed in the 1870s, it is interesting to note how inflated they have become exactly one hundred years later!

This brief commentary and accompanying photographs focus on a few of the more interesting and important Nantucket residences from the whaling era. There are many more that, unfortunately, have had to be omitted but they are all still there for the visitor to see.

The John Wendell Barrett house, 72 Main Street (1820). The early Greek Revival style of this house shows in the pair of slender Ionic columns on the raised portico and in a pilastered observatory (not just a cupola) on the roof *(opposite, top)*. The fine conservative design of this house both outside and inside helped set the pattern for later Main Street residences. John Coleman is believed to have been involved in its design. Like many homes of this period, the house has a double parlor on the right of the entrance *(opposite, bottom)* as well as an additional sitting or music room plus a separate dining room on the left *(above)*. John Barrett was a successful whaling merchant who later became president of the Pacific Bank. During the Great Fire the town officials planned to dynamite the house in order to stop the fire's spread. Mrs. Barrett believed the fire would stop, partly because of the presence of the brick bank diagonally across the street, and she refused to leave the house! Soon the wind shifted and the fire veered to the north along Centre Street. Instead of collapsing after this trying evening, Mrs. Barrett organized supplies of coffee and food for the firefighters.

Above: The Frederick Mitchell house, 69 Main Street (1834). Frederick Mitchell, like John Barrett, was a whaling merchant and later became president of the Pacific Bank. *Opposite, top*: The Charles Coffin house, 78 Main Street (1831). *Opposite, bottom*: The Henry Coffin house, 75 Main Street (1833). Charles and Henry Coffin were sons of Zenas Coffin, one of the wealthiest men in America in the early 1800s. They carried on his business and were the last whaling merchants to close their books. Charles, a Quaker, selected a house with brown trim, whereas Henry had white trim and a cupola instead of an exposed roof walk.

Herman Melville served as a crew member on board the Coffins' *Charles and Henry* during 1842–1843. In 1842, their *Constitution* was the first to use "camels" successfully after a prior attempt had resulted in broken chains and damages to the ship that took a year to repair. The Coffins recognized the importance of the new technique of using camels to float ships over the sandbar at the mouth of the harbor. They worked closely with designer Peter Ewer to correct the problems. Charles and Henry were also public-spirited men, Charles founding the Atheneum library and Henry planting many of the elm trees around town.

The front hall of the Charles Coffin house exudes a warm hospitality with its peach color and sparkling chandelier *(left)*. The front parlor *(above)* is painted a Chinese red, and its secretary, gilded fireplace mirror, and bright chintz are reflective of the Oriental influence on early Nantucket. Both this and the music room *(right)* show the hand of designer Billy Baldwin.

Above: The George Macy house, 86 Main Street (1834), the Job Coleman house, 88 Main Street (*ca.* 1830), and the Matthew Crosby house, 90 Main Street (1829). By the early 1830s cupolas had become popular, as may be seen on the George Macy house above, probably influenced by Henry Coffin's house built across the street the year before. *Opposite, top*: The Jacob Bunker house, 85 Main Street (*ca.* 1725, 1795), the Charles Clark house, 87 Main Street (1830), and the Silvanus Macy house, 89 Main Street (1740, 1800). *Opposite, bottom*: The Sidney Chase house, 82 Main Street (1820). This house shows a simple yet elegant example of a roof walk running the entire length of the house, chimney to chimney.

Above: The Matthew Crosby house, 90 Main Street (1828). This house is very similar to the Thomas Macy II house at 99 Main Street (1770, 1830). Both gentlemen had married Zenas Coffin girls and were thus brothers-in-law of Charles and Henry Coffin. *Left*: The Francis Macy house, 77 Main Street (1790, 1836). In the 1890s a New York journalist, Charles Henry Webb, lived here. He was helpful in arranging the publication of the first short story by his colleague, Samuel Clemens.

The Silvanus Macy house, 89 Main Street (1740, 1800). Silvanus and his brother, Obed, were partners and were instrumental in developing Nantucket's second peak of whaling prosperity in the early 1800s. Upper Main Street from Pine to Pleasant was known as "Court End" in the mid-1800s. Most of the houses were built in the Greek Revival or Georgian style. The Starbucks, Coffins, Macys, Crosbys, Hadwens, Barneys, Swifts, and Swains had such a close family relationship that it was a neighborhood of in-laws.

The Henry Swift house, 91 Main Street (*ca.* 1820). Henry married Mary Coffin, one of Zenas Coffin's daughters, and therefore Zenas had three daughters on Main Street at Nos. 90, 91, and 99, and two sons, Charles and Henry, at Nos. 78 and 75. Bright chintz and flowers make the front parlor a welcome spot *(opposite, top)*. A favorite Nantucket pastime was to sit in the parlor and "watch the pass" on Main Street. The portraits in the dining room *(above)* are of members of the owner's family and are by Gilbert Stuart and John Singleton Copley.

Above: The "Three Bricks" at 93, 95, and 97 Main Street (1836–1838). The identical homes were built by Joseph Starbuck, the most successful whaling merchant of his time, for his three sons William ("East Brick"), Matthew ("Middle Brick"), and George ("West Brick"). With the launching of a new ship, the *Three Brothers*, in 1833 the family had seven successful, consecutive voyages from 1833 to 1865. Matthew became the true successor to his father's business. His house is the only one still in the family (and one of the very few on the island with this distinction at such an age). All three houses are identical, built in the Federal-Greek Revival style, with four end chimneys, granite steps, Ionic porticos, recessed doorways, and square cupolas. These three houses are among the most famous in New England.

Opposite, top: Clement Drew is among the artists represented in the dining room of the "East Brick." Note the colorful, hand-blocked border and the sparkling Tiffany silver.

Opposite, below: The library of the "East Brick" with paintings showing the launching and wreck of the *Joseph Starbuck*.

The front and rear parlors of the "East Brick" have been tastefully decorated with a soft palette of grays, greens, and beige, accented with coral and yellow. The Empire settee *(above)* is believed to have been in the house from the beginning (1837) as have the portraits of the Starbuck children above the piano *(right)*. These rooms are fine examples of making a livable environment out of an old-fashioned, formal setting.

The William Hadwen houses, 94 Main Street (foreground) and 96 Main Street (1840–1845). Hadwen's silversmith and Newport backgrounds are reflected in the refined and bold designs by Frederick Brown Coleman.

Main Street cobblestones. These were brought over from the Gloucester area as ballast and originally laid in 1831. At first they paved lower Main Street to enable the carts to move up to the shops from Straight Wharf more easily. By 1852 they had reached Pleasant Street. The cobbles are warm to the eye but hard on the feet and bicycle. They slow cars down to a proper, leisurely pace.

The Hadwen houses. These represent the culmination of the Greek Revival period—a period of island prosperity reflected in sophisticated architectural design. Soaring columns, recessed porticos, and high foundations were new elements. Frederick Brown Coleman and his brother, John, provided a great influence on the evolution of Nantucket architecture during the peak whaling years. These are the last major houses Coleman built (1845), although the Atheneum was built two years later.

The majestic portico of 94 Main Street with its fluted columns and Corinthian capitals *(above)* and the famous ballroom ceiling *(right)*. The center of the dome could be removed so that dancers could see real stars on a clear evening in addition to the plaster stars or snowflakes on the dome itself. The dance floor was built with barrel-like staves which sprang under the weight of the dancers..

The nautical interests of the owners of 94 Main Street may be seen in the ship models in their rear parlor, overlooking the garden *(right)* and in the painting over the dining room sideboard *(above)*. The ship, painted in 1885, is the *Holkar*, owned by a forerunner of the Cunard Lines and the largest sailing ship in the world at the time. Note the unusual knife boxes on the sideboard and the original hand-blocked wallpaper. Fresh dahlias from the garden bedeck the Boston swan on the table.

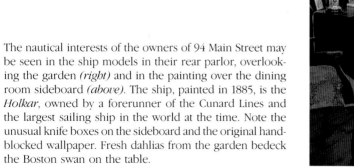

The Hadwen-Satler Memorial, 96 Main Street (1844). The decorative moldings, ceiling rosettes, sliding double doors with silver knobs, and Italian marble fireplaces attest to the prosperity and restrained elegance of mid-nineteenth century Nantucket. In the center of the double parlor *(above)* is a table set with the pink lustre tea service given to Lydia Mitchell when she married John Wendell Barrett in 1816. They both lived at 72 Main Street, the magnificent house she refused to leave when the firemen wanted to dynamite it during the Great Fire.

Above, left: The nineteenth-century garden of the Hadwen-Satler Memorial. *Above, right*: The entrance to the Thomas Macy II house (1830), one of Nantucket's most famous doorways. *Opposite, top*: The Benjamin Coffin house, 98 Main Street (1836). Benjamin was a son of Jared Coffin and built this dignified white house with a front sidewalk of bluestone. In front of the house, at the intersection of Pleasant Street, is a sunken cistern, one of several installed many years ago and fed by rainwater to insure an adequate supply of water in case of another fire.

Opposite, bottom: The Thomas Macy II house, 99 Main Street (1770, 1830). This house was originally built in 1770 by Valentine Swain. Thomas Macy, son of Obed Macy, the historian and uncle of R. H. Macy, added the front section in 1830. The five-bayed facade with an elliptical fanlight and sidelights is one of the most handsome on the island. The fan is blind because the ceiling of the original house behind it was not high enough for a glass window to be installed. The railing that curves out, down the steps, and along the sidewalk has a gentle rounded top. A plain picket fence would not have been acceptable to Macy.

127

Nantucket knockers and nameplates. Silver nameplates were popular on Main Street houses in the 1830s. The graceful brass knockers are a familiar sight throughout the island. The pineapple knocker is on the front door of One Liberty Street, a house built by Benjamin Barney in 1720. Liberty Street was laid out in 1678 and is one of Nantucket's oldest streets. Barney's son-in-law was William Rotch, whose ships were involved in the Boston Tea Party. The Matthew Starbuck house ("Middle Brick") is one of the oldest Nantucket houses still owned by the original family.

The Joseph Mitchell house, 100 Main Street (*ca.* 1730, 1810). Just before he moved into No. 96 Main Street, William Hadwen lived in this two-family house with his partner, Nathaniel Barney. Hadwen and Barney built the brick candle factory now housing the Whaling Museum. Joseph Mitchell later occupied the house. Mitchell went to sea at the age of 14, became a captain at 28, and was particularly successful in the California Gold Rush as a commander of ships rather than a miner of gold. But his whaling voyages were long, arduous, and lonely. He spent the best years of his life on board whaleships, separated from his wife and family.

The Christopher Starbuck house, 105 Main Street (1690, 1753). The oldest part of this house was originally located near Capaum. The afternoon sun provides a warm snoozing spot for the Labrador retriever. The 13-star flag *(above)*, musket, and spinning wheel *(opposite)* provide authentic touches to this early house. The rear gardens are reminiscent of the period.

Opposite: The Capt. David Paddack house, 113 Main Street (1834). *Above*: The James Bunker house, 102 Main Street (*ca.* 1740), one of the earliest houses built with two stories front to back. *Left*: The Capt. Thomas Paddack house, 120 Main Street (1807).

These houses with their flags flying are located near the Civil War monument at the junction of Main, Gardner, and Milk Streets. The monument was erected in 1874 in honor of Nantucket's veterans. The vitrified brick was laid in 1903 as a smoother alternative to the cobblestones.

Above: The Joseph Gardner house on Quarter Mile Hill (1740). This house originally stood next to 153 Main Street. *Right*: The Zaccheus Macy house, 107 Main Street (1748). Macy was a boat builder, and his avocation was that of a physician caring for broken bones. He treated about 2000 cases, and, being a Quaker, never charged for his services.

Above: The Barnabas Gardner house, 153 Main Street (*ca.* 1725). This is one of the oldest houses on Nantucket. Its simple design with a steep shed roof has never been altered with dormers, and no porch or elaborate entrance was ever added to its face. *Right*: The Elihu Coleman house in the original Nantucket settlement of Sherburne (1722). This is the only house remaining in the settlement.

Above: The three-hundred-year-old Jethro Coffin house on Sunset Hill (1686), also known as the "Oldest House." This was built as a wedding present for Tristram Coffin's grandson, Jethro, and Mary Gardner. The lumber came from Peter Coffin's sawmill in Exeter, New Hampshire. Like the Elihu Coleman house, this shows the lean-to style typical of the period: a one and a half story in the front with a long sloping roof to the rear. The houses had a massive central chimney and faced south. *Opposite, top*: The hall of the "Oldest House" was the center for most day-to-day activities. The champfered overhead beam, the eight-foot-wide fireplace, and massive oak lintel are characteristic of early island dwellings. *Opposite, bottom*: The Richard Gardner house, 139 Main Street (*ca*. 1686), built at the same time as the "Oldest House" with a similar layout, lean-to design, and windows imported from England.

Right: The Richard Gardner II house, 32 West Chester Street (1723). This is one of the earliest to belong to a whaling captain and has two full stories. Straight Wharf was built in the same year. The center of town was shifting from Sherburne to the Great Harbor as sheep raising was giving way to fishing and whaling. *Below*: The Matthew Myrick house, 6 Prospect Street (*ca.* 1740)

Above: The Josiah Coffin house, 60 Cliff Road (1724). This was built by a son of Jethro Coffin for his own son. Like his father's and Elihu Coleman's house, this is of the lean-to style and faces south. Nantucketers used a compass to locate their houses, often with extraordinary accuracy. In the late 1880s, Professor Henry Mitchell decided to test the accuracy of this house and calculated the sides would have pointed to magnetic north in 1723. The house was indeed laid out that year. *Left*: The Richard Emerson house on Mill Hill, parts of which date from 1745.

The Nathaniel Macy house, 12 Liberty Street (1723). Like many others, this Nantucket home was moved into town from its original location which, in this case, was near Wannacomet Pond. The timber for these houses was brought over from the mainland, primarily from Exeter, and it was far cheaper to move than to build from the beginning. There were two Sherburnes, the original being west of the present center of town and the new one being the Nantucket we know today. The Nantucket name was adopted in 1795. *Left*: The original kitchen and the west parlor. *Above*: The east parlor is furnished as a dining room with Windsor chairs and other furnishings of the period. Oriental rugs and china reflect Nantucket's early exposure to Pacific trade.

Above: The upstairs chambers of the Nathaniel Macy house. Note the handsome quilt with its bold snowflake design. Both rooms show variations of overhead canopies which were popular at the time.

Opposite: The Benjamin Worth house, 26 Liberty Street (*ca.* 1813). This captain held the record for whaling voyages —almost a million miles, rounding Cape Horn sixteen times and the entire globe twice. He spent a total of 41 years at sea; the aggregate amount of time at home between voyages was about 6 years.

Left: Looking down Gardner Street at Nos. 14, 16, and 18, typical mid-nineteenth-century 2½-story houses. This street was laid out in 1763 by Ebenezer Gardner, whose descendants became prominent whalers by the turn of the next century. One of them, Captain George W. Gardner, started sailing in 1822 at the age of 13 on board a ship captained by his father. He was 29 months at sea on his first voyage and 35 on the next. Because of his youth he had to live in steerage and subsist on salt junk and hard bread. After five years of sailing with his father he was never permitted to eat a meal with him. By the age of 36 he had spent 23 years at sea and a total of 30 months at home between voyages.

Above: A fresh coat of paint on the Reuben Russell house, 45 Centre Street (*ca.* 1830). *Opposite, top*: The Peter Folger II house, 51 Centre Street (1750). This house was occupied by a Folger for almost 200 years. Peter I was a grandfather of Benjamin Franklin. The unusual third story was added in 1815. No other house had a full third story until the Jared Coffin House was built 30 years later.

Above: The Benjamin Chase house, 31 Lily Street (*ca.* 1750). This house was originally built in the lean-to style and located on Fair Street. It was moved to the present site in 1810, and the Greek Revival doorway was added later. *Right*: The dining room and summer porch of the Benjamin Chase house. The pineapple wallpaper and gladiolus in the fireplace show the warm and hospitable touch of the owners.

Above: The old Cottage Hospital was located in these nineteenth-century houses on West Chester Street. When my grandmother stayed here with a broken wrist in 1946 she liked the accommodations so much more than those at the Sea Cliff Inn that she asked if she could stay on for a bit. Business was slow and the nurses were obliging. They gave her in-and-out privileges and a place in front to park her Packard. The nurses lived in the house on the right. The second and third houses from the right contained the hospital and patient rooms.

Left: Bright petunias accent the unusual facade of this house at 16 Lily Street. The entire side opens up to let a summer breeze pass through the house.

The Laban Swain house, 2 Cliff Road (*ca.* 1795). *Opposite, top*: The warm dining room of the Laban Swain house. When we stayed here in the 1960s we had one memorable summer: in August of 1967 there were 27 days of rain. Many evening meals were eaten here long after they had been prepared for family and guests trying to fly in and ultimately taking the late boat. *Opposite, bottom*: The front parlor of the Laban Swain house. The owner made the valance boards and his wife made the crewel curtains before beginning work on the novel seen in the window on the right.

Top: The George Gardner house, 8 Pine Street (1748). When Capt. Paul Pinkham lived here he was keeper of Great Point Lighthouse and was the first to chart the Nantucket shoals—from the tower of the light. *Bottom*: The Ebenezer Drew house, 30 Union Street (1807). Union Street, along with Broad and Centre Streets, has cobblestones quietly napping underneath the macadam. This house is typical of the post-lean-to style: two full stories with two windows on one side of the entrance and one on the other.

Top: The Joshua Coffin house, 52 Centre Street (1756). This was moved in from old Sherburne and, like many other houses of the period, has a secret "Indian Room" carefully concealed within the chimney flue to hide silverware and other valuables from unwanted visitors. *Bottom*: The Obed Macy house, 15 Pleasant Street (1800). Obed Macy was a Quaker historian who wrote the first extensive history of Nantucket in this house. He and his brother, Silvanus, were partners for 47 years in boat building and ship fitting. Rowland H. Macy, who founded a dry goods store in New York, was a grandson of Silvanus and grandnephew of Obed.

Opposite: The Tristram Starbuck house, 12 Milk Street (1784). *Top*: The Capt. Joseph Chase house, 7 Mooer's Lane (1745). *Bottom*: The Prince Gardner house, 9 Milk Street (1740), originally located at Old Sherbune. After the rustic design of the early houses, by the middle of the eighteenth century Nantucket houses were becoming comfortable. But Quakerism was spreading on the island, and its beliefs in plain living, honest work, and simple dress affected Nantucket architecture. The houses were comfortable but not ostentatious. Good craftsmanship was prized over ornamentation. This was the style that prevailed from about 1760 until well into the next century. The ubiquitous gray cedar shingles were prevalent even then.

Above, left: The Thomas Coffin house (also known as the Hinchman House), 7 Milk Street (1810). This house was purchased by Lydia Mitchell Hinchman, a niece of Maria Mitchell and willed to the Maria Mitchell Association in 1944. It now houses their Natural Science Museum. *Above, right*: The Jeremiah Lawrence house (also known as the 1800 house), 4 Mill Street (*ca.* 1807).

The long kitchen of the 1800 House, with its paneled fireplace wall, provides ample quarters for the old pine quilting frame once used on the island. This was often called the "keeping room" and was the center of family activities. Its large hearth and southern exposure meant it was the warmest room in the house. Five rooms are located off this one: two front parlors, one on each side, the small borning room where children were born and cared for when sick, and a summer kitchen.

Above: The west parlor of the 1800 House, set for the afternoon tea. *Opposite, top*: A cozy upstairs chamber in the 1800 House.

Opposite, bottom: The Hezekiah Swain house (also the Maria Mitchell house), One Vestal Street (1790). William Mitchell purchased this house shortly before his daughter, Maria, was born. This view is from the steps of the Maria Mitchell Association Library across the street.

The front parlor and original kitchen of Maria Mitchell's birthplace. She was the first woman to discover a comet, the first woman admitted to the American Academy of Arts, and by 1865 she was the first professor of astronomy at Vassar College, which built an observatory to rival the finest in the nation.

Above: The observatory of the Maria Mitchell Association. The Association was organized in 1902 by Maria's nieces as well as Vassar professors and alumnae. The observatory was built in 1908 and the library, from which this photograph was taken, in 1920 and 1933. *Left*: The little nook at the top of the stairs was Maria's study. There is no computer here—only a few books and a quill pen.

Above and right: The Woodbox Inn, 29 Fair Street (*ca.* 1740). This is one of the island's oldest inns and restaurants.

Opposite: The Joseph Starbuck house, 4 New Dollar Lane (1809). Starbuck was perhaps Nantucket's most successful whaling merchant. He was born around the corner on Milk Street and built this magnificent home in 1809 with an oil house and candle factory at the rear. He also built the "Three Bricks" for his three sons between 1836 and 1838.

Above: The Silas Jones house, 5 Orange Street (*ca.* 1770, 1830). This is is the oldest house on Nantucket with exposed brick ends. Originally the front and back were clapboard. The brick front was added in 1830. *Opposite, top*: "The Block," 15–23 Orange Street (1831). This is the island's only row of town houses and was built by Peter Folger in the same year as his magnificent brick home at the corner of Main and Orange Streets. The first block was occupied by Cyrus Pierce, who founded the Nantucket High School in 1838 with Horace Mann, America's leading proponent of public education.

Opposite, bottom: Looking down Orange Street towards South Tower. One hundred and twenty-six captains once lived on this street over a period of a century—a record unsurpassed by any other street of its length in America.

Opposite, top: The Benjamin Tupper house, 28 Orange Street (1755; 1833). Tupper entertained the famous French historian St. John de Crevecoeur here in 1772. *Opposite, bottom*: The Seth Folger house, 26 Orange Street (1755). The eastern side of Orange Street was called Quanaty or "long hill." The western side of the street was called Wesco Hill. *Above*: The Levi Starbuck house, 14 Orange Street (1838). This handsome Greek Revival house was designed by William Andrews in a massive square style with wooden sides that have flush boards rather than clapboards. It was completed when the last of the "Three Bricks" were built, seven years before the William Hadwen houses.

Top: The Benjamin Easton house, 9 Pleasant Street (1830). *Above*: The Isaac Macy house, 7 Pleasant Street (1825). Both houses were built by John Coleman in the early Greek Revival style with a Doric portico for Easton and an Ionic portico for Macy. John Coleman and his brother, Frederick, were Nantucket's most influential architects in the 1830s and 1840s.

The William Crosby house, One Pleasant Street (1837). This was a wedding gift from Matthew Crosby, who lived at 90 Main Street, to his son and daughter-in-law, Elizabeth Pinkham. Her father was one of the first to chart the Nantucket shoals. It was a fine marriage, and many delightful parties were given by these royal hosts in their new home. They introduced frozen mousse to the island and had the first Chickering piano. Their home was elegantly fitted with French windows, marble mantles, silver doorknobs, and hand-blocked wallpaper. But in 1838 a fire destroyed a number of warehouses where vast quantities of William Crosby's whale oil were stored. The Great Fire almost completely ruined him and the house passed from their hands less than ten years after it was built.

"Moor's End," 19 Pleasant Street (1829–1834). This was the first major brick home built on the island. It was built for Jared Coffin, a successful investor in whaling. Other merchants recognized the social significance of this mansion and soon decided to build their own—all on Main Street. The private garden of "Moor's End" *(opposite)* is the largest walled garden on Nantucket. Also shown are the magnificent dining room with two fireplaces on one side and whaling murals by Stanley Rowland on the other *(above)* and the music room *(left)*.

Above: The front and rear views of "Moor's End." Mrs. Coffin felt that this private estate was too far out of town and persuaded her husband to build an imposing three-story home on Broad Street. *Opposite*: The Jared Coffin House, 29 Broad Street (1845). This house has a raised portico similar to the "Three Bricks" but on a much grander scale. It is imposing even for a hotel, and a cascade of summer roses adds a warm touch.

The interior of the Jared Coffin House. Even though this was the most magnificent home on Nantucket, Mrs. Coffin had grown tired of the island and she and her husband moved to Boston the year after it was completed. It was never again a residence. It reopened the following year as the Ocean House Hotel and is thus Nantucket's oldest inn. It also played an important role in 1870 when the island's economy had reached its ebb. Two men bought it and began to promote tourism to off-islanders. At the same time the Massachusetts Old Colony Railroad decided to promote Cape Cod and the islands. Tourism was well under way in 1872 when the popularity of fishing for blues was discovered, and the Jared Coffin House (then called Ocean House) was thriving. The island we know today is a direct outgrowth of this activity which began over 100 years ago. *Opposite, top*: A portrait of Jared's grandchildren, Seabury, Marianna, and Jared, hangs in the main dining room.

Opposite: The Jared Coffin House (1845). *Top*: The Nantucket Yacht Club, organized in 1890 as the Nantucket Athletic Club and incorporated in 1920. The original part of the clubhouse dates from 1904. *Above*: The Harbor House, which originally opened in 1883 as the Springfield House.

Above and opposite, top: Old North Church or First Congregational Church on Centre Street (1834). This church was built in 1834 and the North Vestry *(opposite, below)* was moved to the rear. The church was expanded in 1850 and the sanctuary ceiling was covered with tin which has now been carefully removed. Construction was completed in 1968 when the familiar spire was added to the tower—dropped by helicopter.

Above: Old North Vestry (1725). This is one of the oldest continuously used church buildings in the United States. It was moved from the edge of town to Beacon Hill, where the "Big Church" stands, in 1765. The original vestry was so well constructed that in spite of the disassembly and move, all of the doors to the pews swung easily on their hinges afterwards. A bell was installed in 1800, the first on the island.

Top: The Unitarian Church on Orange Street (1809), also known as South Tower or Second Congregational Church. *Above*: The interior of South Tower. The famous Goodrich organ was installed in 1831 and is now the oldest American-made organ still in its original setting. In 1843 Carl Wendt, a Swiss fresco artist who introduced trompe l'oeil painting to America with the decoration of the old Treasury Building in Washington, painted the magnificent interior. It is therefore one of the oldest trompe l'oeils in this country. He used a subtle palette of warm and cool grays, providing a baroque touch to the church, which is now being carefully restored.

The bell in this tower was purchased in Lisbon in 1812 but hidden on the island until after the war. It was hung in 1815 and rung by hand until 1957, when it was electrified. The custom of ringing three times a day began in 1811 with the Revere bell in Old North Church, first only at night to warn people to return to their homes. Later, it was continued three times a day and in 1848, when the South Tower bell and clock became the official timepiece for the town, the practice was transferred there. Today the bell rings exactly 52 times. No one is sure why but probably it is because that is approximately three minutes' worth, and it was easier for the bell ringer to count strokes than watch a clock.

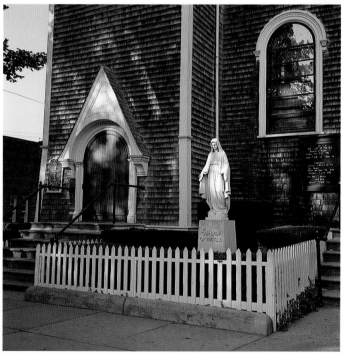

Opposite: The Methodist Church on Centre Street (1823). The pediment with its handsome dentil molding and six plain Ionic columns is believed to have been added by Frederick Coleman in 1840. Soon after the church was built its cellar was used to store whale oil. *Above*: The Baptist Church on Summer Street (1841). The present bell, weighing 1600 pounds, was cast in Troy, New York, and installed in 1854. This is perhaps Nantucket's prettiest church, with graceful, unpretentious lines. It was designed by Frederick Coleman. *Left*: Saint Mary's Catholic Church on Federal Street (1896).

The Old Gaol on Vestal Street (1805). This is the oldest of its kind in New England. Built in the style of a log cabin, it has logs for walls, ceilings, and floors that have been bolted together with iron straps. Oak planks cover the interior walls and floor of the cells—and one cell is sheathed with iron straps for solitary confinement. In the early 1800s when Nantucket had a bustling waterfront, the jail was well occupied, especially by brawling sailors who met in the grog shops. Imprisonment for debt was common then, too. One man was sentenced for six months after stealing a coat. The jail was last used by the town in 1933.

The Old Mill (1746). Originally there were four mills on Mill Hills or Popsquatchet Hills. This one was designed and built entirely by one man, Nathan Wilbur. It is held together with hickory wood pins; nails were too expensive then and bolts were unheard of. The top rotates into the wind with the help of a fifty-foot mast, which follows a stone track on the ground. Canvas sails are added to the blades to help catch the breeze. A brake activated by an oak beam and heavy stones keep them from turning too fast.

Early morning at the Old Mill. This is the oldest mill still grinding corn in America. It is a tribute to good, basic design and craftsmanship that this mill and many other structures on island are fully operable over 200 years later.

Five

Around Nantucket

Getting around Nantucket has not always been as easy as today by car. In fact cars were not permitted on the island until 1916. When Clinton Folger brought an Overland from the mainland in 1913 in order to deliver the mail to 'Sconset, he was forced to tow it to the Milestone Road with horses before he could proceed on the state highway. (Occasionally, he motored through town in the winter and was arrested for defiance.) We could have used the same system during World War II. I vaguely remember getting our car to the island but not being able to use it after that due to a shortage of gasoline coupons. So transportation for us was with a horse and buggy or a scooter, and of course the beach bus. We did take the car to Wauwinet on occasion which was such an exciting adventure that my sister, age five, would sing a somewhat repetitive ditty: "Going to Wauwinet" (those were all the lyrics) from Cliff Road until we passed the "Casino." My brother first learned to drive on one of these Wauwinet beach excursions with our father acting as "driver ed."

My family first came to Nantucket fifty years ago. My father was recuperating from an accident, my grandfather had died after a long illness, and so it was decided that a summer on Nantucket would do everybody some good. They all piled into my grandmother's Packard, including Clara the cook, and set off. Whatever luggage that could not fit on the top or back went up via Railway Express and had its own leisurely tour of New England. My family took a relaxing trip to New Bedford with the car on the overnight boat from New York. With a crew of two hundred and a chandeliered dining room as grand as the Pierre Hotel's, the Fall River Line's *Priscilla* was indeed a pleasant way to begin a Nantucket journey in the 1930s. At New Bedford they transferred to the *Nobska* and had a stateroom. Even when the *Nantucket* went into service many years later my father always booked a stateroom for the crossing. We could spread out, and there was always a steward to bring a bucket of ice when the bell was pressed.

The Connecticut Turnpike and the *Uncateena* changed all that but only heightened the anticipation of spotting the lights of Nantucket from the sound. One evening crossing on her first visit, my sister-in-law said she wasn't sure if she was seeing the lights of Nantucket up ahead or the stars of heaven. "Was there a difference?" she then asked. No, there really wasn't.

Included in the pages that follow are views of all the outdoor activities that have made Nantucket special to us over the years: patio lunches, beaching, golfing, sailing, and hiking on the moors. Please take your time now; there's a lot to see.

Alfresco Activities

Summer dining alfresco at the Jared Coffin House *(above)*, the bandstand in Harbor Square *(opposite, top)*, and on Old South Wharf *(opposite, bottom)*. The bandstand is also the location of summer concerts on Sunday evenings.

187

Above and opposite: Dining at the White Elephant Hotel, Nantucket's only harbor-front inn and cottages. Guests can watch the steamers and other ships from the deck or pool.

A shiny Steinway inside catches the reflection of the patio's awning and guests.

The Nantucket summer porch is the supreme spot for quiet enjoyment and relaxation. The porches have become favorites with visitors and natives since the turn of the century. Shown here are porches of the White Elephant Hotel *(above)*, a private residence on Main Street, and a yacht in the harbor *(opposite)*.

Above: Yellow umbrellas lend a festive touch to the Yacht Club patio. *Opposite*: Harbor views from inside the Anchorage.

Bright sand and big, bold umbrellas have been a trademark of the Cliffside Beach Club for generations. The club is the successor to a beach club first established in 1864.

Above: "A tisket, a tasket, a green and yellow...." Summer baskets for sale in their maker's garden. *Right*: Wall Street, next stop.

Archery practice at the Nantucket Boys' and Girls' Club. This organization provides evening and weekend activities for youngsters between the ages of 7 and 18. It plays an important role in establishing values and shaping the lives of its 400 members.

Above: Moor's End Farm, one of Nantucket's few remaining vegetable farms and nurseries and certainly the one with the oldest produce wagon.

Opposite: Old North Cemetery on New Lane.

Old North Church is a familiar landmark from many points on the island. This is the view from North Liberty Street.

Two of Nantucket's golf courses, Siasconset *(top)* and Sankaty Head *(above)*. The Nantucket Golf Club on Cliff Road has been closed for many years and its clubhouse is now occupied by the Nantucket Conservation Foundation. For a while the Nantucket Golf Clubhouse was a residence owned by Gladys Wood, who rented it to our family in the early 1960s.

Sailing Day

Sailfish, Sunfish, and Day Sailers provide everyone with a chance to get out on the water.

Nantucket harbor is a sailor's delight. There is always a breeze. Whether alone, with your best friend, or a family group, a quiet afternoon on the water is the perfect tonic to help forget your cares.

Best friends get together for a summer sail whether they be a spaniel on a Sunfish, or a professional crew on a schooner. The Opera House Cup race *(above)* has matched wooden-hulled ships against each other since 1972. Originally there were 12 participants—10 from Nantucket and 2 from the Vineyard. Most recently there have been 75. All must have wooden hulls at least 32 feet in length.

Above: Neither rain nor fog will keep these sailors home—when there's a Yacht Club race. The Yacht Club presently has nine classes of boats.

Opposite: Heading out to sea through the jetties. These massive stone walls were first proposed by the U.S. Congress in 1803 to help keep sand from accumulating across the entrance to the harbor. Various opinions and indecision resulted in no action being taken until 1881, well after the whaling industry had ended. In 1842 when the sandbar had become too high, camels or floating drydocks were introduced to transport the whaleships high in the water. The camels were sunk low enough for the vessel to pass over the chains joining them. Then the water in the storage tanks was emptied by steam power, and the floating system could support 800 tons and draw only seven feet. The term "camel" is believed to derive from the Middle Eastern practice of placing a load too heavy for one camel between two of them and letting it be supported from the camels' sides. Nantucket camels were last used in 1849. The western jetty was built in 1881 and the eastern one in 1894. Five hundred thousand tons of stone were delivered by barges that year.

The Beaches

Nantucket has 55 miles of beaches surrounding the island. Some face the sound's calm waters and are favored by all age groups. A popular spot with our family is Step Beach off Cliff Road *(opposite)*. For more adventurous surfing, Cisco Beach on the South Shore is the place *(above)*.

Beaches on the sound include Capaum
(above), site of one of the original Nantucket
settlements in 1659, neighboring Dionis
(right), and the popular Jetties *(opposite)*.
Capaum means "enclosed harbor," and Dionis
was the wife of Tristram Coffin.

The Jetties Beach offers calm waters for swimming, a broad beach that is an easy bike ride from town, a chance to practice windsurfing, and panoramic views to capture on canvas or film.

Above: The colorful umbrellas of Cliffside Beach Club. *Opposite*: The view from on top of the cliff at the head of Step Beach. Steamers and other ships form a steady parade as they line up to enter and leave the jetties guarding the harbor entrance.

Cliffside Beach Club has been a popular private bathing club on Nantucket's North Shore for generations. Its colorful umbrellas, clean white sand, and weathered boardwalks are inviting. The Ford station wagon has never left the island since it first arrived here 40 years ago.

These bright umbrellas capture the sun's rays and glow with color against a blue summer sky. They offer a sheltered spot for friends and visitors to circle around and have a gam.

Sails and other sights around Nantucket harbor.

224

Summer artists have many opportunities to capture views of the island and its visitors on canvas and film.

Sandcastles are popular everywhere whether they be inspired by Aztec or Babylonian design, Barcelona's Gaudi, or a childhood fantasy.

Above: Surfside Beach is an easy bike ride from town. *Opposite*: A game of paddle at Tristram's Landing in Madaket. Both Surfside and Madaket were subjects of proposed land developments in the 1880s that never materialized. The Surfside plan was more successful due to Henry and Charles Coffins' backing the first railroad to Surfside in 1881 and their purchase of a large hotel in Rhode Island, transporting it on seven barges, and reconstructing it at Surfside in 1883. But winter storms eroded the railroad bed and service became increasingly unreliable. A new line to 'Sconset proved trustworthy and 'Sconset became the center of attraction. By 1887 the Coffins' 100 Surfside lots were sold at auction for $2.80 each, the hotel was boarded up, and eventually the sea reclaimed everything.

An evening ride along the beach at Miacomet *(opposite, top)* and a romp at Madequecham Beach *(opposite, bottom)*. Miacomet means "place where we meet" and Madequecham means "foothill place." *Above*: Summer seashells at Hulbert Avenue Beach.

Ponds, Forests, and Moors

No Bottom Pond off West Chester Street. The many fresh water ponds on Nantucket are the work of a glacier which originally formed the island as a moraine and later became surrounded by rising waters along the coastal plains.

Mallard ducks at "Hollywood Farm" in Polpis *(top)* and at Consue Spring *(bottom)*. The duck pond at Hollywood Farm serves as one of several reservoirs for the windswept Cranberry Bog. Consue Spring on Union Street in town is partially the result of the construction of a railroad grade across the marshland in 1881, which can be seen across the top of the photograph.

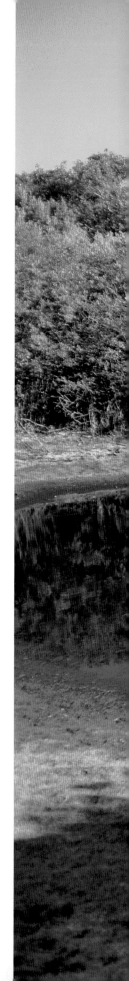

Hidden away in the moors are some of the island's loveliest jewels. There are two ponds near Sesachacha simply called the "Mirror Ponds" that are popular with deer and other wildlife for their calm, clear spring water *(top and opposite)*. There are also three "Foot Ponds," one of which is called "Donought Pond" because of its island *(above)*. Many people flying to the island from Boston have seen this one near Altar Rock.

Above: Long Pond from the Crabbing Bridge at Madaket. *Opposite, top*: Quaise Pond off Bassett Road. Quaise means "at the place of growing reeds." Although this lies in the morainal portion of the island, it is too shallow to be considered a kettle hole pond. The large boulders are glacial erratics left behind by the melting glacier about 15,000 years ago. *Opposite, bottom*: Capaum Pond, near Dionis on the North Shore. Capaum means "enclosed harbor." This was originally a cove, open to the sea, and was thus the site of one of the island's first settlements. Heavy storms and moving sand closed this little harbor, forcing the settlers to relocate around the Great Harbor of present-day Nantucket.

Left: Gibbs Pond, in the center of the Cranberry Bog property. John Gibbs (also known as Assassamoogh) was a Nantucket Indian, a minister, and a Harvard graduate. The Nantucket Indians were part of the Wampanoag tribe, which settled in lower Massachusetts. Gibbs Pond is the island's second largest fresh water pond after the East side of Hummock Pond. Long Pond and Sesachacha Pond are brackish in part.

Opposite: Squam Pond, near the Atlantic ocean and halfway between Quidnet and Wauwinet. Squam means "beautiful water."

Opposite, top: Maxcy's Pond near the junction of the Cliff Road and Madaket Road. The fresh fish, calm waters, and private bathing beach make this little pond popular with all types of visitors including Canadian geese. *Opposite, bottom*: Pest House Pond in Shimmo. Originally those with communicable diseases were treated at this quiet spot across the harbor from town. Shimmo means "a spring," Shawkemo means "middle field of land," and Monomoy means" rich soil." *Above*: One of the two "Wigwam Ponds" near Altar Rock. This is a kettle hole—steepsided with no stream in or out. Eventually it will become a bog. There are 10,000 acres of moors on Nantucket, unique in this part of the world. They are covered with heath plants, bearberry, broom crowberry, bayberry, and shadblow. Sun, fog, and the warmth of the Gulf Stream combine to give these plants all the nourishment they need. To stand on Altar Rock and look in any direction is to experience wonderful isolation in an endless landscape. There are no houses, trees, or other objects to intrude on the carpet spread out as far as the eye can see.

242

Opposite: The headquarters and familiar marker of the Nantucket Conservation Foundation. The Foundation's main purpose is to conserve, preserve, and promote public enjoyment of plants, birds, and other wildlife. *Above*: Queen Anne's lace and a weathered cedar fence. What could be more typically Nantucket?

Above: Golden asters on Tuckernuck. These bloom along the side of the roads from mid to late August. *Opposite, top*: A mallow rose at Capaum Pond. This is a member of the hibiscus family. It grows next to ponds and blooms during August in various shades of light pink to deep rose. There are so many at Squam Pond that it is often referred to as Mallow Pond. *Opposite, bottom*: A summer bouquet of Queen Anne's lace. Nantucket has a greater variety of vegetation than any other spot of similar size in America. Many of her plants have been imported—heath and broom from Scotland, ivy from England, even rugosa roses from Japan.

The head of Hummock Pond looking towards Swain's Farm. The Nantucket Conservation Foundation and the Land Bank Commission have acquired 300 acres on this side of the pond lying between the Madaket Road and Ram Pasture. This area was one of the island's first settlements and for many years was an important spot for sheep grazing.

The Shawkemo Hills. Glacially deposited material forms a moraine consisting of kames (hills) and kettles (valleys), and occasionally ponds like the Wigwam Ponds. Shawkemo means "middle field of land."

247

Madequecham Valley, south of the Milestone Road and east of the airport. Madequecham means "foothill place." This heathland epitomizes the island's beauty and isolation. Heaths, or "moors" as they are commonly called, are unique in this part of the world. The ground cover is dominated by members of the *Ericaceae* family: bearberry, low bush blueberry, and huckleberry. Also present are bayberry, false heather, sweet fern, and scrub oak. A rare and extremely shy Philadelphia or wood lily grows in the valley, too, but once its bloom is picked nothing can cause it to bloom again. Many birds find homes here—owls and hawks as well as sparrows, gold finches, and a variety of songbirds.

During the fall, Nantucket's moors form an undulating carpet of reds, browns, and greens. This is part of the island's kame and kettle (hill and valley) landscape. Shown here are huckleberry (red ground cover), scrub oak (mounded plants), and eastern red cedars (the taller evergreens in the middle right of the photograph).

Ram Pasture, a 625-acre tract between the eastern and western sections of Hummock Pond. This was the Conservation Foundation's first major purchase. The name derives from the grazing land that became an an important part of Nantucket life in the early years. Today the area is rich with bearberry, broom crowberry, bracken, and small wildflowers. It is also a favorite feeding area for duck, geese, tern, and other waterfowl from the Atlantic flyway.

Above: The moors in fall, looking toward Altar Rock, one of the highest points on the island. On the horizon at the left is the tip of the white "omni," an airport navigational aid. This heath was once a major sheep grazing area, covered with huckleberry, bearberry, and golden heather. *Opposite, top*: The island's two major cranberry bogs, built initially in 1865, are the world's largest. In the fall they become lakes of wine-red fruit. The berries were known to the Indians and also whaling captains who kept a few barrels on board to help curb scurvy. Today the berries are harvested by flooding the bogs, letting the vines float, and paddling the berries loose. They float to the surface and are corralled by pontoons before being scooped out. *Opposite, bottom*: A foot-driven paddler is seen in the upper part of the photograph preceded by a guide checking the soil for holes. The berries in the foreground are sharp enough to pick, attesting to the strength of this camera's lens.

The forest at Squam Swamp. This is not really a swamp, but rather a densely vegetated hardwood forest with many low-lying depressions which collect rainwater in shallow pools. The plants in the photograph are typical of forested areas: swamp maple, tupelo, and cinnamon fern. Squam means "beautiful water." Nantucket's forests are mostly hidden away, and abound with white-tailed deer, quail, pheasant, and rabbits. It is interesting to note that there are no squirrels, chipmunks, foxes, skunks, porcupines, or raccoons anywhere on the island.

Above, right: Nantucket's famous Hidden Forest, a private spot in Polpis not open to visitors. *Above, left*: The Pine Forest along the Milestone Road. Many of Nantucket's trees have been imported. Henry Coffin was responsible for most of the graceful elm trees along Main Street. He also imported, in 1875, over 30,000 Scotch pines and fir, as well as 10,000 larch trees. It is possible that the island's abundant Scotch heather and broom came over at the same time.

Almanac Pond, near Folger Hill. It is said that the severity of the upcoming winter can be predicted by the amount of water in the pond.

A cascade of summer roses covers this typical 'Sconset cottage.

Six

Siasconset and the Other Villages

"Did you ever hear of 'Sconset where there's nothing much but moors, And beach and sea and silence and eternal out-of-doors? . . . ." This little village described by Bliss Carmen has the distinction of being situated furthest out in the Atlantic Ocean. It illustrates how much its original inhabitants wanted to get away from the rest of the world. 'Sconset and another fishing community to the north, Sesachacha, were among the first settlements on the island (about 1675). In fact, Mitchell Coffin's "Auld Lang Syne" *(274)* is thought to have been built in that year and therefore would be eleven years senior to Jethro Coffin's "Oldest House."

The cluster of houses along 'Sconset's east bank had a modest beginning as one-room fishing shacks. All cooking was done outside, and the overall spartan, camp-like atmosphere was appealing to the men. Eventually, their women began to drive out from Nantucket town to visit and were also drawn to its simplicity. But to live there required some sprucing up of the rustic fishing cabins. The first round of additions were "warts," tiny bedrooms added to one side of the house which at first glance appeared minute but in actuality were more spacious than the average ship's cabin.

Next came a room on the opposite side of the house which was called a "porch" but in reality was the kitchen. All of these modest homes were constructed out of secondhand items. Lumber, doors, and windows were carted out from town and assembled in a great mixture of materials. One wart on the "Martin Box" *(268)* was originally an old boat house, while the northern wing of the John Morris house began life as a hay shed.

At the same time the mainland was celebrating its independence from England, 'Sconset was celebrating its liberation from the rain barrels—with the drilling of its first well in 1776 *(285)*. With this the village began to thrive. By the 1830s and 1840s, it was a popular spot for whaling captains and their crew to visit when they were home from a voyage. It offered a needed respite from the unfamiliar bustle of life in town.

The railroad, however, changed all that. The line was first built to Surfside which experienced a short-lived development boom in the early 1880s. But winter storms eroded the tracks to such an extent that passengers were often derailed en route. The line was straightened out in 1899 and 'Sconset became the destination. The village then experienced its own development explosion and became Nantucket's Newport. Large fashionable summer houses were built for the townspeople who wanted to get away for a while. They preferred a more spacious and stately style of home to the dwarf fishing shacks. This was fine with the theatrical set from New York who, thanks to Edward Underhill's promotions, began to discover the little "doll houses" and who were enchanted with the idea of crawling in and out of doorways and bending down to clean out the wart gutters.

The story of 'Sconset is one of isolation and quiet retreat. While Nantucket has gone through various stages of growth and prosperity, the simplicity and solitude of 'Sconset has remained essentially the same throughout—interupted only on occasion, such as when the young David Sarnoff and his colleagues were operating the first wireless station in the country here in the early 1900s. (He subsequently retired from this job and established R.C.A.)

As for the fate of neighboring Sesachacha, which was settled at the same time as 'Sconset and at one point was a larger village, no one really knows. It was just that much further to get to and gradually the townspeople preferred to cluster around 'Sconset. Some of the houses were moved down and the rest were abandoned. "Shanunga" *(271)*, whose oldest section dates from 1682, was originally a Sesachacha fishing cottage. (At various times this house has been a store, an inn, and tavern, and even the village post office, beginning in 1873.)

Today 'Sconset peacefully naps in the warm summer sun and the sweet sea air, her little shingled cottages gray with the salt of the sea wind and covered with blankets of roses in July. There is no other place on earth quite like it.

Above: "The Captain" and *Left*: "The Corners."

Top: The Swain cottage on the Polpis Road and
Left: The George Gardner house (1740).

"Snug Harbor" (1780). 'Sconset roses thrive on the special blend of sunshine and fog that prevails during the early summer.

Above: "Eagle Cottage," being recorded by a visiting artist from Marblehead. *Opposite, top*: "Seldom Inn." This says it all. *Opposite, bottom*: "Hedged About" is encircled by an eight-foot hedge trimmed to perfection.

Top: A summer windowbox on "Roof Tree" (1780). *Bottom*: "The Maples" (1800). *Opposite, top*: "Heart's Ease" (1815). *Opposite, bottom*: "Castle Band Box" (1814). 'Sconset started out as a fishing village when the good fishing grounds for cod and flounder were discovered a short distance offshore. Many of the cottages built further north around Sesachacha (now Quidnet) were moved to 'Sconset in the early 1800s, some not so successfully. One cottage called "High Tide" became a pile of seasoned lumber when the tide went out and it collapsed.

Left: "Eagle Cottage" (1789). *Below* and *opposite*: "Martin Box" (1720). The flag is slightly larger than the door. This cottage has matured over the years and now has a cozy living room with a fireplace and wicker rocking chairs as well as a formal dining room. The bedrooms are small but comfortable.

Above and *opposite*: "Shanunga" (1682). This is perhaps the oldest house in 'Sconset although its neighbor "Auld Lang Syne" (1675) may be the oldest building. "Shanunga" has also served as a store and a post office as well as a tavern. During the turn of the last century 'Sconset became a popular destination for young couples to go for an evening, visiting Betsy Carey's pub (this same house) and returning by carriage in the late hours. Her tavern had become popular when it was discovered that the ice she sold contained a strong flavor of rum. *Opposite, top*: The charred upright beams on either side of the bed indicate the earlier presence of a large kitchen fireplace. The same flue now serves the living room *(above)*.

Top: The Captain Valentine Aldrich house, 6 Elbow Lane (1753). *Left*: "Dexioma" (1780).

Top: "Nauticon Lodge" (1734). This little cottage has rooms built like staterooms, with narrow doorways, and a single large living room which has been described as hardly enough to contain a small family seated. *Above*: "Wanackamack" (1815).

Opposite: "Auld Lang Syne" (1675) is the oldest building on Nantucket. It has a large living, dining, and sleeping room plus a kitchen wart on the north and a small storage wart on the west. It has been changed very little over the past three centuries. *Above*: "House of Lords" (1753).

Above and *opposite, top*: "Pomme de Mer" is covered with bright red roses during the summer. The living room is large and informal, a perfect spot to unwind from the tempo of city life. *Opposite, below*: The Wade Cottages, one of 'Sconset's two hotels, *avec Deux Chevaux*.

Somewhere under here are cottages belonging to the "Summer House," a popular inn and one of 'Sconset's two guest houses. Roses and tiger lilies make staying here a bit like sleeping in a garden.

"Two If By Sea" is the name this Concord family has given their 'Sconset cottages. Red and white roses have been covering 'Sconset cottages for almost 100 years. They bloom from late June to late July along with white and yellow daisies. Also shown is a veil of silver lace on the barn.

Top: The "Little House" (1885). *Right*: "Doll House" (*ca.* 1895). These are two of the houses owned by Edward Underhill in the early 1900s. He had three streets of rental houses including an extra room on wheels that could be dragged around to a rental family with numerous members. He made his houses small—replicas of the early cottages—with low eaves and ladders leading up to children's sleeping lofts. Soon 'Sconset became an extension of New York's famous acting community, the old Lamb's Club. But gradually air-cooled theatres put an end to their long summer vacations.

A turn-of-the-century advertisement for Siasconset once read as follows: "The farthest at sea of any point on the Atlantic Coast, it is also the nearest the Gulf Stream. Here one has all the emotions of living at sea without the disagreeable effects of sea-sickness... For wholesome and delightful bathing, the waters are unequalled... The purity of the air and the light, porous soil assure freedom from malaria. Persons suffering from hay-fever are exempt from the ailment during their stay. The climate is especially adapted to those who suffer from insomnia or nervous prostration... The visitors at Siasconset are intelligent, cultured and refined. They come for rest, retirement and recreation."

Two gray Nantucket ladies: a 1931 Plymouth roadster calling on a 'Sconset bluff house. This car has been in the same family for three generations. Down from the bluff is a long stretch of beach facing the Atlantic Ocean on which grounded whales were first discovered. Apparently this happened more than once because the Indian name of Siasconset means "place of many whale bones."

Union Chapel (1886), 'Sconset's only church, has both Catholic and Protestant services at separate times on summer Sundays.

Top: The Old Bridge at 'Sconset (1887) and the famous but former sun dial. It's 11:00 A.M.

Bottom: The 'Sconset pump (1776). The town's first well was dug the same year the Declaration of Independence was signed.

The Chanticleer Inn (1909), one of the island's most famous restaurants *(above)* and downtown 'Sconset with the post office and a restaurant *(opposite)*. The first wireless radio station in North America was built here and operated by the *New York Herald*. It was later taken over by the Marconi Company. By 1901 messages were being transmitted from Cunard Lines to its New York offices via little 'Sconset, an otherwise sleepy hamlet that did not receive its own village electricity until 1925.

Top: A private cabana at the Sankaty Head Beach Club looking out at the Atlantic from the bluff.

Bottom: The Sankaty Head Golf Club, with views of its challenging course, built in 1921.

The 'Sconset Casino (1900), primarily a tennis club. The Casino was opened with great fanfare on August 4, 1900, at an evening celebration that included selections by the 'Sconset Hungarian Orchestra, two short plays, Japanese and Spanish dancing, and a Negro song and dance. Ladies were requested to remove their hats during the performance and special trains were scheduled to bring people back afterwards. By 1909 the Casino had six tennis courts and two bowling alleys. It had begun tennis matches with Nantucket and won the first round in 1907. Movies began in 1915 with a hand-cranked projector (which was stopped every 20 minutes in order to thread a new reel), a piano for suspense music, and hard seats. Nothing much has changed.

Along the Milestone Road are some of the island's many daffodils, standing at attention and waiting for the annual Daffodil Day parade. Over *one million* bulbs have been planted in the last decade. This has been undertaken by the citizens of Nantucket under the initial sponsorship of the Nantucket Garden Club and represents one of the largest such projects in America.

The best way to get to 'Sconset is by convertible, hopefully with someone else driving. This is the Commonwealth's first state highway with a separate bicycle path. Travel was not always so luxurious, however. By the 1870s the 'Sconset road had deteriorated to the point where some of the coaches lost their wheels in transit.

Wauwinet,
Polpis and
Quidnet

The Wauwinet skyline. This collection of nineteenth and twentieth century houses extends from Squam up to the head of the harbor. It is the furthest removed community on the island, and its residents prefer it that way.

Opposite: The Wauwinet House was built at the turn of the nineteenth century and is thus one of the island's oldest inns. When I was growing up we called it the Casino. It is shown basking in a sea of July daisies at the water's edge. *Above*: Gray cedar shingles and boardwalks across the dunes lend a warm, informal touch to this little community with the sea at its back and the harbor in its lap.

Opposite: Sailing and sunning on the harbor side of Wauwinet, named for one of the two chiefs on the island in 1659. The beach is edged with a wrack line of eel grass. *Above*: Quidnet means "at the point." This community is nestled on the north side of Sesachacha Pond and in some respects is older than 'Sconset. Bathers have a choice of the calm waters of Sesachacha or the challenges of the Atlantic, each separated by only a few yards of sandy beach. Sesachacha means "blackberry grove."

Top: Polpis means "divided harbor" and is the only harbor on the island where trees grow down almost to the water's edge.

Above: The magnificent cliffs of Pocomo may be seen from Shimmo and further down the harbor on clear days. They require quite a few steps to mount *(opposite)*.

A fishing shack and dried cedar driftwood dot the shore-line of Coatue. This is a popular sailing destination across the harbor from town, with plenty of scallop and other seashells. Coatue means "at the pine tree place."

The Nantucket Lifesaving Museum, built in Quaise as a replica of the original Surfside station (1874). Despite the lighthouses, built and supervised by the United States Government since 1789, and the charting of the shoals, ships still continued to run aground. Several refuge houses were built on the island in the late 1700s by the Massachusetts Humane Society. The oldest remaining structure of this organization is the boathouse on Maskeget, built in 1883. The United States Life Saving Service, founded in 1868 on the New Jersey coast, merged with the Revenue Cutter Service founded by Alexander Hamilton when he was Secretary of the Treasury, to form the U.S. Coast Guard in 1915. It is the only such service under the Department of the Treasury auspices.

Madaket

The original nine settlers on Nantucket first landed in 1659 at Madaket. Their leader and island patriarch for many years was Tristram Coffin. Although Madaket went largely unsettled for the next 300 years, a new community called "Tristram's Landing" was developed in the 1960s along the lower section of Long Pond and White Goose Cove. The gray shingles of these multiple-ownership homes enable them to blend into the environment now.

Madaket is best known for fishing (surfcasting at the point or sailing out of Hither Creek's boat yard). It is a simple community of cottages on the sand dunes, a place to put your feet up and relax. Madaket means "sandy soil at land's end."

The Outer Islands

Opposite: Esther Island. *Above*: Whale Island. These are Nantucket's newest islands. Esther was once called Smith's Point. Three houses and a car were left behind when hurricane Esther rudely broke through one evening. Now the sand is accumulating and is calling Esther back to Madaket. It may no longer be an island anymore, at least for awhile. Whale was originally part of Tuckernuck, which in turn was part of Nantucket many years ago.

Tuckernuck means "loaf of bread" and it is Nantucket's largest satellite island. It once was connected to the mainland and was a popular spot for cattle grazing. DeCrevecoeur mentioned Tuckernuck in his *Letters from an American Farmer* in 1782 as an ideal location for raising turkeys, chickens, and cattle because there were no foxes or wolves to prey on them. Farmers were able to move their livestock and produce back and forth to the mainland along the south shore and across what are now Whale and Esther Islands.

Tuckernuck is a private island owned by its summer residents. Visit is by invitation only. There were permanent residents as early as 1770. In 1829 there were 11 houses on the island, and there are 26 today, along with a few old cars and jeeps in various stages of retirement. There is no electricity on the island and only emergency radio telephone service. That's just the way owners want it.

Muskeget means "grassy land" and is Nantucket's other main satellite island. It has always been a separate island, and today has two buildings and a jeep. Shown here is the boathouse of the Humane Society, built in 1883. During the eighteenth and nineteenth centuries the Humane Society maintained several shelters on Nantucket to aid those involved in shipwrecks.

Brant Point Lighthouse. This perky structure is a familiar sight to everyone who rounds the point on the steamer. It is also the spot for tossing two pennies overboard when departing the island in order to assure a speedy return.

Brant Point is the site of the second lighthouse ever built in America, 1746. Only Boston's Beacon Light is older. At night it shines a red light, which may be seen in the photograph above. Also shown is the boathouse of the United States Coast Guard which maintains Nantucket's lighthouses. The red occulating lamp (this means it is on more than off) can be seen for 10 miles. Red marks the starboard or right side of the channel entering from seaward. The cycle is four seconds: three on and one off.

Sankaty Head Light (1848). The lamp is 158 feet above sea level and has a nominal range of 29 miles. There are actually four lamps making a complete rotation every 30 seconds and therefore a flash appears every 7.5 seconds. The image of 'Sconset bluff is reflected in the silver dish of the light and is therefore reversed. The view is looking south, so the Atlantic Ocean should be on the left side.

Top: Sankaty bluff is the highest point on the island, 111 feet above sea level, surpassing Altar Rock at 103 feet and Folger Hill at 109 feet. Sankaty means "cool bluff."

Right: Brant Point Lighthouse. This present structure was built in 1904 and has a twin at the entrance to Hyannis.

"Two pennies overboard and come again soon!"

Index

GLOSSARY OF INDIAN NAMES

Nantucket Indians were members of the Wampanoag people. The following interpretations are based on a 1910 article by Henry Barnard Worth, "Nantucket Lands and Land Owners," in the Vol. II Bulletin of the Nantucket Historical Association. Some of the translations have been verified and some have not. Therefore these are not definitive translations but rather are the popular meanings that have been guessed at over the years.

Capaum	Enclosed harbor	Quidnet	At the point
Coatue	Pine tree place; place of sharp points	Sankaty	Cool bluff; around the bluff
Coskata	Place of broad woods	Sesachacha	Blackberry grove; place of dark berries, snakes
Hummock	One of the sachems or chiefs	Siasconset	Place of the great bone or many bones (referring to whale bones)
Madaket	Poor i.e., sandy soil; land's end	Shawkimo	Middle field of land
Miacomet	Place where we meet	Shimmo	A spring
Monomoy	Rich soil	Squam	Beautiful water
Muskeget	Grassy land	Tukernuck	Loaf of bread
Nantucket	Land far out to sea; faraway island	Wanacomet	Good field
Nobadeer	Good fishing grounds	Wauwinet	One of the sachems
Polpis	Divided harbor	Wesco	At the white stone
Quaise	Place of tall reeds		

ACKNOWLEDGMENTS

Production Supervision: Peter H. Grant, Tsuguo Tada
Printing Consultation: Takeshi Fukunaga, Ronald Hill, Yoshiyasu Kosugi, Kaoru Shinzaki
Publishing Coordination: Starling R. Lawrence

Approximately 90 percent of the photographs have been taken with medium-format Roleiflex cameras using Ektachrome film. The balance has been with a Nikon camera and Kodachrome film. I am indebted to Gene Mahon and his staff at the Camera Shop for their valuable assistance as well as to Russell Kern at Eastman Kodak Processing Laboratories, Inc. I am equally indebted to Scott Anderson, Mimi Beman, Patti Clafflin, Tom Dickson, Bob and Dotti Tonkin and their respective colleagues for their suggestions about the book and to Mr. and Mrs. Thomas Amory, Miss Rita Ayer, Mr. and Mrs. Tony Bischof, Mr. Rick Blair, Mr. and Mrs. Dudley Darling, Mrs. Henry Greenleaf, Mr. and Mrs. Charles Kilvert, Mr. and Mrs. Peter Krogh, Mr. and Mrs. John Lodge, Mr. and Mrs. James Taylor and Mr. and Mrs. Stephen West for permission to photograph their lovely homes. Credit for the Opera House Cup Race photograph on page 207 goes to Cary Hazelgrove and the daffodils on page 290 to Rick Blair. Some of the artists photographed include Marilyn Chamberlain, Tom Dunlay, Sybil Goldsmith, Beverly Hall, Candace Lovely and Chin Manasmontri. To the many other people who have been associated with this project I would like to express my sincere appreciation.